TESSA BRA

*seasonal
recipes*

TESSA BRAMLEY'S

seasonal recipes

I recall that the first time I heard about Tessa Bramley's cooking was when I was Editor of the Good Food Guide. What was mentioned most often was her use of herbs and home-grown produce. Some cooks used to pop a decoration on the plate for effect but not many integrated flowering herbs into their whole method and style. Tessa was different. She chose with an eye for taste; she used discretion. The Old vicarage became a place where you could tell the time of year by what was on the plate. It followed the seasons; it enhanced each fugitive month as thyme flowers followed tansy and sweet cicely lay beneath balls of deep yellow ice cream. Tessa Bramley puts all this into her book far better than I can ever express it.

Tom Jaine

MEREHURST

PHOTOGRAPHY BY MICHELLE GARRETT

Paperback edition published 1996 by
Merehurst Ltd
Ferry House, 51-57 Lacy Road, Putney,
London SW15 1PR
Copyright © 1995 Tessa Bramley

First published in hardback in 1995 as
The Instinctive Cook

ISBN 1 85391 692 7

A catalogue record of this book is available
from the British Library.

The right of Tessa Bramley to be identified
as the Author of this Work has been asserted
by her in accordance with the Copyright,
Designs and Patents Act 1988.

Managing Editor: Gill MacLennan
Edited by Rosemary Moon
Cover design by Bill Mason
Design/Art direction by Pene Parker
Photography by Michelle Garrett
Styling by Pene Parker

Food for photography by Tessa Bramley

Typesetting by Servis Filmsetting Ltd
Manchester

Colour separation by Fotographics Ltd U.K.
Printed in Italy by G Canale & C SpA

For Peter & Howard

With grateful thanks to my mum for her continuous faith in me and to my son and business partner Andrew without whose help, encouragement and taste this book could not have been written.
His support throughout has spurred me on. Thanks also to Justine and to my dedicated and talented kitchen team whose enthusiasm in testing the recipes has been boundless. It has been a very happy experience and for that I am grateful to my managing editor Gill MacLennan for suggesting that I write the book in the first place and for her enthusiasm and patience whilst I did so. Pene Parker for her beautiful design and Michelle Garrett for her stunning photography also deserve my gratitude.
We have had a lot of fun putting it together. I do hope you have as much fun cooking from it.

My late husband Peter, my son Andrew and I started the Old Vicarage at Ridgeway as a family business, having first cut our teeth on a little lunchtime Bistro. We bought the building at auction in 1986 in a desperate state of repair. The gardens were, however, magnificent, the surroundings idyllic and we all fell in love with the comfortable old house. We had very clear ideas from the outset as to how we, were we customers, would probably like things to be done. We tried to exclude our own personal dislikes whilst emulating good restaurants we had enjoyed in Britain and abroad. We began to gain recognition in the press and food guides and, more importantly, we gained a loyal following of good customers; lovely people who were both helpful and encouraging in our early days.

As our reputation grew we gained the confidence to start developing our own personal style. The thrill of being 'in the ratings' was immensely satisfying, but nothing compared to the glow gained from the thanks and praise of appreciative early customers. I shall never forget them, for I owe my success entirely to their support. Many restaurant goers are not aware that simply saying 'Thank you – we enjoyed that' is a tremendous boost to the cook. Mine did – and I tried harder as a result.

introduction

This book is about seasonal country cooking driven by the garden and nature. It is about honest cooking with pure flavours and food with a natural balance and harmony. Seasonal produce does taste better than out-of-season food, yet in our multi-national society it is foolish today to ignore both produce and cooking styles from other countries.

Ideas, fads and trends will come and go, for food is fashioned by the way we live. Yet the old ways should not be lost. My interest lies in taking the better ideas and adapting them to our modern lifestyles.

Of course there is very little in cooking which is new. Looking back through our culinary development in the last few centuries, there have been major foreign influences introduced as a result of Britain's role in world trade and politics. These influences were not just from our nearer European neighbours but from Africa, the Middle East and Asia too. Many have become part of the backbone of our traditional country cooking and are now totally absorbed into our food culture having been accepted as being British.

Everyone can develop ordinary cooking skills into something very special with practice and taste. It is the putting together of flavours which is important and not the technique, for most cooking skills are very simple. There is immense satisfaction in working things out for yourself. From that you evolve a style but the secret of keeping that style fresh is to always be questioning and seeking to improve what you do. ➡

'Cooking is my passion, my favourite relaxation and my first love.'

FRONT COVER
Gazpacho, Fresh saffron tagliatelle with young spring vegetables, Fillet of wild salmon steamed with elderflowers & muscat sauce

LEFT
Glazed Apple Tarts

'Beautiful, fresh ingredients are so satisfying to handle.'

Cooking is immensely therapeutic after a stressful day and even though I do it for a living, it is still my favourite way to unwind. Beautiful fresh ingredients are so satisfying to handle. To turn them into an interesting meal, however simple, is an act of love and joy if you have an appreciative audience to murmur approval. What could be better than eating the fruits of your labour with family and friends?

'Blending flavours and occasionally bending the rules is a lot of fun.'

Don't be afraid to try the recipes in this book. If you follow the instructions one step at a time, they will work for you. Some approaches and techniques I use are unorthodox yet I find that they work well for me. Do remember, however, that recipes are merely a guideline to inspire you to do your own thing. As you gain in confidence, your own style and taste will take over and you will interpret them in your own way, mixing and matching ideas. Blending flavours and occasionally bending the rules is a lot of fun. Just keep an open mind, relax and keep tasting! Even if your opinions do not coincide with mine at least I might set you off on your own voyage of discovery. We should not have to tread the middle path with food and the way we cook it or put up with compromise. Let's do what we really enjoy – why simply refuel at the table when we can excite and delight? It is often the simplest and most spontaneous food with brilliant ingredients which is memorable.

'Why simply refuel at the table when we can excite and delight?'

I fell into this profession through a clear desire to cook. I have enjoyed various experiences in my transition from catering college to home economist, to teacher, to keen amateur family cook and then on to professional chef and restaurateur. These changes have taught me to look at cooking from varying perspectives. I hope this book breaks down for you some of the mystique surrounding professional chefs and their work environment. Its raison d'etre is for all cooks who love food; amateurs who cook purely for the enjoyment of it and want to get the best out of themselves in the kitchen. I have always adopted a simple attitude towards my craft with no fuss, no pretension and a very open mind. I count myself lucky to be able to live with my job and to combine a successful business with my passion, my favourite relaxation and my first love – cooking.

ABOUT THE RECIPES

Read a recipe right through before starting to cook. There are many interesting serving suggestions given at the end of the recipes which will help you to decide what to serve with each dish.

A standard spoon measurement is used in all recipes.
1 teaspoon = one 5 ml spoon
All spoon measures are level, unless otherwise stated clearly in the recipe.

Ovens should be preheated as specified.

Eggs used in the recipes are size 2.

Quantities are given in metric and imperial measures for all recipes. Follow one set of measures and do not mix them as they are not interchangeable.

contents

spring

summer

autumn

winter

spring

Cooking in spring has a freshness and liveliness about it after the robust earthy flavours of Winter.

Tiny shoots of fresh green herbs appear, the first to show in my garden are lemon balm, sorrel, chives and chervil. Forced rhubarb with its clear pink stems and fresh flavour is one of the first fruits. During March and April I think of rod caught wild salmon, with a sorrel butter sauce; lemon tarts; golden corn fed chickens and primroses. It is a youthful time; a time of crisp young vegetables and lighter cooking. Succulent Spring lamb becomes available, so good it tells its own story and sea trout leap with the salmon.

roast rack of lamb WITH A CHERVIL
& LEMON CRUST

SERVES 4

2 racks of young spring lamb
salt and ground black pepper
extra virgin olive oil

CRUST:
4 lemons
2 cloves garlic
125 g (4 oz) fresh breadcrumbs
4 tablespoons chopped fresh
chervil
2 tablespoons chopped fresh
French tarragon
2 tablespoons chopped fresh
chives
2 eggs

SAUCE:
300 ml (10 fl oz) lamb stock
(page 141)
1 small glass Madeira
sprig tarragon
chilled unsalted butter

What could be a better herald of warm spring days than the new season's lamb, combined with the fresh light taste of spring herbs? Chervil and French tarragon both have a sweetish aniseed flavour and light green feathery leaves. Irresistible!

Ask your butcher to remove the chines and French trim the rib bones, but to give you back the bones and trimmings for stock.

1   Preheat oven to 200C (400F/Gas 6).

2   Skin and trim racks if your butcher has not prepared them for you. Remove all the outer layer of fat. Trim cutlet bones right back to eye of meat, cutting fat away between bones and scraping bones clean. This is called French trimming.

3   Season racks. Heat a little olive oil in a large frying pan and sear meat on all sides. Remove with two slotted spoons.

4   Prepare crust. Grate lemon zests, crush garlic and mix with the breadcrumbs, chervil, tarragon and chives.

5   Beat eggs in a wide, shallow bowl and dip in outer edges of racks. Press crumb mixture onto eggy surface and place racks, crumb side uppermost, in a roasting tin. Drizzle with olive oil.

6   Roast in preheated oven for 12–14 minutes, until meat is pink (but not blue!). Rest lamb in warming oven for 5 minutes before carving.

7   Make a sauce while lamb is resting. Reduce lamb stock with pan juices and Madeira, stirring up any crusty bits. Add a sprig of tarragon. Finish by swirling in some chilled butter until sauce is viscous enough for you – the exact amount will vary – the more butter you add, the thicker the sauce.

8   Carve racks into cutlets and serve with sauce poured round.

Pommes Anna (page 144) make a very good accompaniment to this simple spring roast. Serve Annas in centre of plates with cutlets resting on them and sauce poured round.

spiced fillet of beef WITH HOT

SMOKED PEPPERS

SPICED BEEF:
thick cinnamon stick
2 pieces star anise
1 teaspoon coriander seeds
1 teaspoon mustard seeds
1 teaspoon black peppercorns
1 piece fillet of beef,
weighing about 220-250 g (7-8 oz)
salt and pepper
extra virgin olive oil

SMOKED PEPPERS:
1 red pepper
1 yellow pepper
olive oil infused with rosemary
and chilli

SPICED DRESSING:
2 tablespoons extra virgin olive oil
1 teaspoon balsamic vinegar
1 teaspoon soy sauce
1 piece stem ginger
4 spring onions
salt and ground black pepper
reserved spices
fresh Parmesan, to serve

Use generously heaped measures of spices for a good, full flavour. Serve the beef with Cucumber Relish (see page 150) and Horseradish Cream (see below).

1   Using only half cinnamon stick, combine all spices and grind coarsely in a pestle and mortar or a grinder. Reserve a pinch of spices for the spiced dressing.

2   Trim beef of all fat, sinew and skin. Season and rub with a little olive oil. Press spices over beef, leaving two cut ends free.

3   Heat a griddle or heavy cast iron frying pan to an evenly hot temperature. Sear beef on all sides for 2 minutes each side (except two ends). The outer part of beef will be cooked and middle rare.

4   Place beef in a small, deep container. Pat back any spices which have fallen off and pour some good olive oil over beef. Leave until cold then cover and chill overnight in the refrigerator. This will allow flavours to infuse.

5   Roast peppers and remove skins (see page 30).

6   Set up a smoker (page 25) and smoke peppers over a few sprigs rosemary for 2 or 3 minutes.

7   Remove core and seeds from pepper and cut flesh into long strips. Dress with a little olive oil infused with rosemary and chill until required.

8   Prepare a dressing for beef by mixing together 2 tablespoons olive oil, balsamic vinegar and soy sauce in a small bowl. Finely shred ginger. Trim and chop spring onions. Add to dressing with seasonings and reserved spices from beef. Whisk all ingredients together.

9   Slice beef very thinly and serve with the smoked peppers. Pour a little of spiced dressing over beef and top with shavings of fresh Parmesan.

HORSERADISH CREAM
If you have fresh horseradish root, grate a 5 cm (2 inch) piece. Place in a small saucepan and cover with cold water. Bring to boil then drain. Mix blanched horseradish with a little cream, seasonings, sugar and chopped fresh chives. If you are using a jar of horseradish sauce, whisk 3 tablespoons double cream into 1½ tablespoons horseradish until it is light and fluffy. Adjust seasoning and stir in chopped fresh chives or 2 or 3 finely chopped spring onions.

corn fed chicken WITH LEMON,

GINGER & CORIANDER

SERVES 4

2 slices fresh root ginger
2 fat cloves garlic
1 lemon
2 × 1 kg (2 lb) corn fed chickens
1 tablespoon seasoned flour
extra virgin olive oil
1 small onion
1 leek
1 stick celery
850 ml (30 fl oz) white chicken
stock
1 pinch saffron strands
1 bunch fresh coriander

A chicken dish with fresh flavours and the colours of spring.

1 Preheat oven to 180C (350F/Gas 4).

2 Blanch ginger (see page 29). Cut into thin strips, about 1 cm (½ inch) long. Cut one and a half cloves garlic into equal sized pieces. Pare zest from the lemon and shred.

3 Using a sharp knife cut down either side of chicken breastbones, letting rib cage guide knife to remove chicken breasts. Cut legs and thighs together from carcasses. Make carcasses into white chicken stock (page 141).

4 Make incisions with tip of a small knife all over chicken breasts and legs. Insert alternating pieces of ginger, garlic and lemon zest.

5 Toss chicken in seasoned flour, shaking off excess. Heat a little olive oil in a frying pan and sear chicken on all sides. Remove to a casserole dish.

6 Finely chop onion. Trim leek and chop white part only. Trim and chop celery and crush remaining piece of garlic. Fry all vegetables in pan with remaining blanched ginger.

7 Squeeze juice from the pared lemon and add to pan with a little stock, scraping up any crusty pieces from base of pan. Gradually add remaining stock and saffron. Bring to boil.

8 Pour vegetables and stock over chicken in dish and cover with a lid or foil. Bake in preheated oven for 40–45 minutes. Test thighs with a skewer. Chicken should feel very tender and juices run clear.

9 Remove chicken to a plate using a slotted spoon. Keep warm.

10 Pass chicken liquor through a fine sieve into a clean pan. Press vegetables firmly with back of a ladle to extract all juices and flavour. You should now have a bright yellow sauce packed full of flavour with the consistency of single cream. If you prefer a thicker sauce, whisk in a little olive oil which, in any event, will enhance flavours.

11 Arrange chicken pieces on a serving dish. Add 2 tablespoons chopped fresh coriander leaf to sauce and adjust seasoning if necessary. Pour sauce around chicken. Garnish with a few coriander leaves.

seared salmon fillet WITH

SORREL BUTTER SAUCE

SERVES 4

1 piece salmon fillet, about 750 g
(1½ lb)
salt and ground black pepper
extra virgin olive oil
7.5 cm (3 inch) piece cucumber
2 leeks
150 g (5 oz) unsalted butter

THE SAUCE:
300 ml (10 fl oz) fish stock (page
140)
squeeze lemon juice
piece star anise
large handful sorrel leaves
sugar, to taste

When the first of the wild salmon appears in the markets it is a delight not to be missed. Although it is quite expensive, compared to its farmed counterparts, there is nothing quite like the firm texture and mother-of-pearl pinkness of the wild fish.

Cook wild salmon simply but with due reverence – it is a treat! The salmon season usually coincides with the new sorrel growth in our garden. What could be better than salmon, crisp on the outside and meltingly moist in the middle, with the fresh, clean flavour of sorrel sauce?

1 Preheat oven to 200C (400F/Gas 6).

2 Skin and bone salmon fillet. Cut into four pieces. Season and rub top side of flesh with olive oil.

3 Heat a dry cast iron pan or a griddle until evenly hot. Sear salmon, oiled side down. Do not attempt to move fish until a crisp golden surface has formed, at which point salmon will lift easily out of pan with a palette knife. Moving fish too soon will leave flakes sticking to pan, including your crispy topping, and spoil the presentation.

4 While fish is cooking start sauce. Place stock in a saucepan with lemon juice and star anise. Boil until reduced by half.

5 While sauce is reducing, shred cucumber into strips. Trim and finely shred leeks. Melt 30 g (1 oz) butter in a pan, add cucumber and leeks and stir-fry briefly until just softened. Strew vegetables over base of an ovenproof dish and arrange salmon pieces on top.

6 Bake in preheated oven for 3 to 5 minutes, depending on thickness of salmon, until just cooked. Fish will be firm to touch yet with a pearly pinkness in middle.

7 While salmon is in oven, finish sauce. Whisk remaining butter, a little at a time, into pan to thicken sauce and give it a gloss. Remove star anise and season to taste.

8 Roll up sorrel leaves and shred finely with a sharp knife – this is called a chiffonade.

9 Add fish juices from ovenproof dish to sauce. Serve salmon fillets on a little cucumber and leek mixture on each plate.

10 Stir sorrel chiffonade quickly into sauce at last moment and check seasoning; add a little sugar if necessary. Sorrel will turn bright green and give a citrus flavour. Pour sauce around salmon – serve immediately, or colour will be lost.

Buttered new potatoes and a spring vegetable stir-fry would balance this well, without detracting from the clarity and simplicity of the flavours.

filo parcels of crab, SPRING ONION & GINGER WITH sweet and sour

PEPPER SALSA

SALSA:
1 small red pepper
1 small yellow pepper
2 tomatoes
1 courgette
1 green chilli
1 shallot
1 clove garlic
2 tablespoons sunflower oil
1 lime, rind and juice
1 teaspoon sesame oil
salt and ground black pepper

FILO PARCELS OF CRAB:
1 piece fresh root ginger
375 g (12 oz) white crab meat
2 sticks lemon grass
8 spring onions
salt and cayenne pepper
1 teaspoon soy sauce
1 tablespoon chopped fresh coriander
90 g (3 oz) unsalted butter
8 sheets filo pastry about 18cm × 9cm (6 inch × 3 inch)

Serve two filo parcels per person. Smaller crab filo parcels would make attractive drinks party snacks.

Cook your own crab for this recipe, or buy from a reputable fishmonger who will cook and dress the crab for you. Such men are like gold dust and well worth nurturing. Serve with Sweet and Sour Pepper Salsa, a chunky sauce with a freshness of flavour, just slightly sweet and sour. Serve the Salsa warm.

1 Prepare the Salsa. Roast and skin peppers (see page 30). Dice half of each pepper – keep remainder for use in salads.

2 Skin tomatoes (see page 48). Cut in half, remove cores and scoop out seeds with a teaspoon. Dice tomato flesh.

3 Trim and dice courgette. Cut chilli in half and remove core and seeds. Finely chop half flesh. Peel and chop shallot. Crush garlic.

4 Heat sunflower oil in a small pan, add shallot, garlic and chilli. Fry until softened but not brown. Add courgette and cook for just a few seconds until it turns bright green.

5 Remove pan from heat and add lime rind and juice and sesame oil. Season and leave for at least one hour for the flavours to infuse before use.

6 Prepare the filo parcels. Preheat oven to 220C (425F/Gas 7). Blanch root ginger (see page 29).

7 Check through crab meat to make sure that there are no pieces of shell in it.

8 Trim lemon grass and remove outer leaves. Use tender white part only and chop finely. Trim and slice spring onions.

9 Cut root ginger into thin slices, then into fine matchsticks (Julienne).

10 Combine crab meat, ginger, lemon grass and spring onions in a small bowl. Add salt and pepper, soy sauce and coriander. Season to taste.

11 Melt butter. Cut one sheet filo in half to give two square shapes. Brush each with melted butter and place one over other, giving it a quarter turn so that there are 8 points to filo. Repeat with remaining sheets of filo, giving eight star shapes. Keep unbuttered filo covered to prevent drying out.

12 Place a little of crab meat in centre of each filo star. Collect up sides and gather over filling, giving a little twist to form shape of an old-fashioned money bag. Place on baking sheet and brush with remaining butter.

13 Bake in preheated oven for about 15 minutes, until crisp and golden. Warm Salsa and serve with filo parcels.

SERVES 4

RHUBARB BUTTER SAUCE:
500 g (1 lb) young forced rhubarb
1 teaspoon caster sugar
150ml (5 fl oz) fish stock (page 140)
3 pieces star anise
salt and ground black pepper
30 g (1 oz) chilled unsalted butter

4 fillets of brill, about 180 g (6 oz) each
150 ml (5 fl oz) white wine and water, mixed

TEMPURA:
125 ml (4 fl oz) chilled water
1 egg
1 scant tablespoon plain flour
8 large scallops with roe
sunflower oil, for deep-fat frying

Japanese tempura needs to be executed perfectly. Experiment with temperatures of cooking oil and get to know the right batter consistency. As with most things, practise makes perfect! The result should be a light, crisp, almost transparent coating which will not mask even the most delicate of ingredients. Try making tempura of spiced vegetables, prawns and pieces of assorted fish for a very elegant, light starter.

tempura of scallops WITH BRILL

ON A RHUBARB BUTTER SAUCE

Rhubarb and gooseberry sauces are peculiarly old English ways of enlivening oily fish such as mackerel. I find fruit sauces particularly elegant with shellfish too. Give it a try – you'll be surprised!

1   Preheat oven to 220C (425F/Gas 7).

2   Trim rhubarb and cut into slices. Place in a saucepan with sugar and 1 tablespoon water. Cook slowly to a purée.

3   Bring fish stock to boil in another pan and boil until reduced by half. Add rhubarb, 2 pieces star anise and seasonings. Simmer for 2 or 3 minutes then pass through a sieve into a clean pan.

4   Reheat sauce, adding chilled butter to give a good gloss. Season to taste, adding a little extra sugar if necessary. Keep sauce warm – not hot; that will spoil its colour.

5   Heat oil in deep fryer for tempura.

6   Skin brill fillets if fishmonger has not already done this for you. Season fish and lay each fillet on a sheet of foil two and a half times its size. Fold foil over fish to make a parcel and seal two short sides.

7   Crush remaining piece of star anise into wine and water and pour mixture into parcels through the top. Seal up.

8 Place foil parcels on a baking sheet and cook in preheated oven for 4–6 minutes, dependent on thickness of fish. When cooked it will feel firm to touch but have a pearly, opaque look.

9 Whilst brill is cooking make scallop tempura. Whisk chilled water and egg together with a pinch of salt until very frothy. Quickly whisk in flour.

10 Test fryer for temperature. It will need to be around 180C/350F.

11 Dip scallops in frothy batter and deep fry for 1½–2 minutes until crisp and golden. Drain on absorbent kitchen paper.

Serve brill with tempura of scallops on a bed of vegetable spaghetti and flat beans with sauce poured round.

12 Remove brill from oven. Pour fish juices into rhubarb sauce. Taste sauce and season if necessary. Whisk a little more butter into sauce if necessary to thicken.

fresh saffron tagliatelle WITH

YOUNG SPRING VEGETABLES

SAFFRON TAGLIATELLE:
saffron stamens
280 g (10 oz) plain flour
1 teaspoon salt
1 tablespoon extra virgin olive oil
1 egg
4 egg yolks

SPRING VEGETABLE SAUCE:
30 g (1 oz) pine kernels
3 sprigs fresh rosemary
180 g (6 oz) small courgettes
120 g (4 oz) spring onions
60 g (2 oz) mange tout
1 tablespoon olive oil
300 ml (10 fl oz) double cream
120 g (4 oz) small broad beans
(shelled weight)
120g (4 oz) asparagus tips
salt and ground black pepper
chopped fresh chives, chive
flowers and rosemary, to garnish

This makes a delightful fresh starter in the late Spring with all the fresh greens of the new season's vegetables. The pasta should be dried for about one hour before cooking.

1   Prepare saffron tagliatelle. Put a pinch of saffron stamens in a small bowl and add 3 tablespoons boiling water. Leave to cool, to infuse colour and flavour. Strain through a fine sieve.

2   Place flour and salt in a food processor; add oil, egg and egg yolks. Start motor and gradually add saffron infusion through feed tube. Stop processing as soon as the dough holds together.

3   Turn dough onto a lightly floured work surface and knead until shiny and smooth. Wrap in foil or plastic wrap and chill for at least one hour.

4   Cut dough in half and roll each piece very thinly. Cut into strips about 60 cm (24 inch) long. Dry slightly then cut into tagliatelle. If you have a pasta roller, roll dough to setting 6, then cut into tagliatelle. Dry strips on rolling pins or a new broom handle.

5   Prepare spring vegetable sauce. Toast pine kernels until golden under a hot grill or in a heavy dry frying pan. Chop rosemary. Slice courgettes. Trim spring onions but leave whole. Top and tail mange tout.

6   Bring a large pan of salted water to the boil and add 1 tablespoon olive oil.

7   Place rosemary and cream in a large pan. Bring to boil and reduce slightly. Add broad beans and asparagus tips and cook for 30 seconds.

8   Add spring onions, courgette rings and mange tout. Cook for a further 30 seconds.

9   Stir in pine kernels.

10 Add tagliatelle to pan of boiling water, return to boil and cook for just thirty seconds. Drain, rinse and add to vegetables and cream.

11 Season to taste and heat through. Serve immediately garnished with chopped fresh chives, chive flowers and a sprig of rosemary.

sea trout, LIGHTLY SMOKED OVER FENNEL

WITH A CHIVE SAUCE

1 sea trout, about 1.75 kg (3½ lb)
salt and ground black pepper
extra virgin olive oil
2 handfuls fennel fronds

CHIVE SAUCE:
1 shallot
1 bulb Florence fennel
15 g (½ oz) unsalted butter
150 ml (5 fl oz) fish stock
150 ml (5 fl oz) dry white wine
150 ml (5 fl oz) double cream
fresh lemon juice
2 tablespoons chopped fresh
chives

Sea trout, or salmon trout, are actually brown trout which have left the river to run with the salmon out to sea. They look similar to salmon but are, in fact, quite different. The flesh is pink in colour with a sweet flavour and a much softer texture. Sea trout are available only for a very short time, so use them whenever you get the opportunity.

Ask your fishmonger to fillet the sea trout but to leave the skin on.

1 Preheat oven to 200C (400F/Gas 6).

2 Cut each fillet of sea trout in half. Using tweezers remove as many bones as you can feel with your fingertips. Season trout lightly and rub olive oil into skin.

3 Set up a smoker (see below). Strew grid with lots of fennel fronds. Smoke fish, skin side down, for 2 minutes. Turn fillets and smoke for a further 1 minute – 3 minutes in all.

4 Place some more fennel fronds in a roasting tin. Remove trout from smoker and set in roasting tin, skin side uppermost. Rub skin again with olive oil.

5 Prepare sauce. Finely chop shallot. Trim and finely chop Florence fennel. Melt butter in a saucepan and cook shallot and fennel until soft but not brown. Add fish stock and wine. Bring to boil and reduce by half. Add cream and reduce again to desired consistency. Season to taste and add a few drops of lemon juice if flavours need sharpening up a little.

6 Place fish in preheated oven for 2 or 3 minutes to heat through and finish cooking.

7 Add chives to sauce at last moment. Serve sea trout with chive sauce poured round.

Smoking the sea trout until cooked right through would dwarf the delicate flavour of the fish, so the final cooking takes place in the oven. This gives just a delicate smoked flavour. The chives are added to the sauce at the last moment to give zest and immediacy to the sauce. This would be lost if they were added too soon.

SETTING UP A SMOKER: to improvise a smoker you will need a roasting tin plus its lid, or another matching tin to sit on top. Set tin on the hob and strew base with woody herbs, vine cuttings, apple wood or whatever flavourings you are using. Place a wire rack in and cover with lid. Wait until a steady stream of smoke emerges from the sides between the top and bottom tins, then add the food to be smoked. Turn heat down, keeping smoke constant.

roast barbary duckling WITH

ROSEMARY

SERVES 4

**2 × 1.75 kg (3½ lb) oven ready
Barbary ducklings
salt and ground black pepper
1 onion
1 carrot
1 stick celery
2 stems rosemary
honey**

Ask your butcher for the livers when you buy the ducks – they flavour a wonderful risotto (page 28) which is perfect with roast duckling. Serve with a crisp green salad.

1 Preheat oven to 200C (400F/Gas 6).

2 Cut duck legs from carcass at hip joint. Season lightly.

3 Wash vegetables but do not peel. Chop roughly. Place in a roasting tin to form a trivet. Lay duck legs on vegetables, skin side up.

4 Roast legs in preheated oven for about 35 minutes, until they are cooked through and skin is crispy.

5 Using game shears or robust kitchen scissors cut away remaining carcass, leaving breastbone with two breasts attached.

6 Make a slit in each breast, near breastbone, and insert a sprig of rosemary. Season lightly.

7 Heat a cast iron frying pan or skillet until evenly hot (see page 53). Sear duck breasts in hot pan. Remove breasts to roasting tin with legs, smear breasts with a little honey and roast for 15 minutes.

8 Rest breasts in a warming oven for a further 10 minutes.

9 Cut breasts away from bone with a sharp, flexible filleting knife. Cut down beside breast bone, then allow knife to travel along rib cage to remove breasts. Save breast bone and all trimmings to make stock for freezer (page 140).

10 Serve roast duckling with risotto of duck livers (page 28).

De-glaze roasting tin with a glass of red wine, scraping up all meat sediment, and add flavoured wine to stock made from bones.

risotto of duck livers WITH

SUN DRIED TOMATOES & GREEN OLIVES

SERVES 4

20 halves sun dried tomatoes
30 g (1 oz) pine kernels
livers from 2 ducks or 4 large
chicken livers
milk, for soaking
salt and ground black pepper
1 onion
2 fat cloves garlic
5 tablespoons extra virgin olive oil
225 g (8 oz) arborio or risotto rice
good pinch saffron stamens
1 yellow pepper
1.1 litre (2 pints) duck stock (see
page 141)
4 stems oregano or golden
marjoram
24–30 green olives
15 g (½ oz) unsalted butter
2 tablespoons Madeira
2 tablespoons chopped fresh
chives

Shake the pan rather than stirring while cooking rice – this helps to keep the rice whole, rather than breaking up the grains. Risotto should not be allowed to become dry or to stick to the pan. It should be creamy and the grains – lightly chewy, but without any hardness in the middle.

If serving this risotto with Roast Duckling (page 26), pile risotto onto plates and stand a crispy duck leg up in the centre of each portion. Slice the duck breasts diagonally (from skin to fillet) and surround the duck leg with overlapping slices of duck breast and the duck livers from the risotto. Spoon the juices over.

Risotto seems to go with summer weather and easy entertaining. This risotto is punchy and flavoursome in its own right. With the duck and liver juices allowed to drip into it, it becomes sensational. A crisp green salad is all that is needed alongside.

If your butcher is unable to supply you with duck livers use fresh chicken livers. These are also available in most supermarkets.

1   Skin sun dried tomatoes. Cover with boiling water and leave for 10 minutes. Drain, rinse under cold water and peel away skins.

2   Toast pine kernels under a hot grill or in a dry frying pan until golden.

3   Trim livers, removing any green bits. Soak in a little milk for 15 minutes, to remove any trace of bitterness. Rinse in cold water and pat dry. Cut in half and season lightly.

4   Peel and finely chop onion. Peel and crush garlic. Heat olive oil in a large frying pan or risotto pan, add onion and garlic and cook until soft.

5   Add rice and saffron. Stir well until rice is thoroughly coated and has absorbed oil. Season lightly.

6   Cut pepper in half, remove core, seeds and membrane. Finely dice flesh. Add to pan.

7   Gradually add half stock. Bring to boil. Reduce heat to a slow simmer and cook until rice is almost done. Keep adding a little more stock, shaking pan frequently.

8   Strip leaves from oregano or marjoram and chop. Add to pan with olives and sundried tomatoes after rice has been cooking for 10 minutes.

9   Add toasted pine kernels after a further 2 or 3 minutes.

10 Melt butter in a hot frying pan. Fry livers briskly on all sides turning frequently. Make sure that they are cooked but still quite pink in middle. Add Madeira to pan and scrape up any meat residue into it.

11 Season risotto to taste and add chopped chives.

12 Serve risotto with livers piled on top. Spoon liver juices over and allow them to mix into rice.

Thai spiced fish cakes

SERVES 4 AS A STARTER

FISH CAKES:
225 g (8 oz) potatoes
100 g (4 oz) salmon fillet, skinned
100 g (4 oz) monkfish tail, skinned
1 green chilli
4 coriander seeds
1 lime
1 tablespoon chopped fresh coriander leaf
1 tablespoon chopped fresh chives
salt and ground black pepper
4 tablespoons sesame seeds
2 tablespoons sunflower oil
2 tablespoons sesame oil

SAUCE:
1 piece fresh root ginger
1 small onion
1 small clove garlic
2 limes
2 Kaffir lime leaves
150 ml (5 fl oz) fish stock (page 140)
150 ml (5 fl oz) double cream
½ teaspoon sugar
salt and white pepper

To blanch fresh ginger peel the root and cut ginger into thin slices. Drop them into a small pan of cold water and bring to the boil. Drain ginger and throw away water. Repeat this process twice more. This removes all excess bitterness and will leave only the pure ginger flavour.

Sesame seed oil gives extra flavour during frying and the sunflower oil raises the frying temperature to give a crisper finish to the fish cakes.

The exciting flavours of the Pacific Rim give a twist to fish cakes as we know them! Any firm fish could be used. Ask your fishmonger to skin the fish for you although, if you forget, it is very easy to do at home, so long as your knife is sharp. Serve with Lime and Ginger Sauce.

1   Prepare fish cakes. Peel and chop potatoes. Bring to boil in a saucepan of salted water, then simmer until soft. Drain and mash potatoes.

2   Now prepare sauce. Blanch root ginger (see below). Drain and shred finely. Peel onion. Finely chop half for this recipe. Peel and crush garlic. Grate zest from one lime and squeeze juice. Cut peel from remaining lime and cut fruit into segments. Shred lime leaves.

3   Place chopped onion, garlic and lime juice in a small saucepan with fish stock and one shredded lime leaf. Simmer until onion is soft. Set to one side.

4   Now return to the fish cakes. Heat a little water in a frying pan. Add salmon and monkfish and poach until just cooked. Remove fish from cooking liquor and flake.

5   Cut chilli in half and remove core and seeds. Chop flesh finely. Crush coriander seeds and sieve to remove husks.

6   Grate zest from lime into a bowl. Mix the potato, salmon, monkfish, chilli, coriander seeds, lime rind, fresh coriander and chives. Season to taste – you may need to add a squeeze of juice from the lime to liven up flavours.

7   Shape into 8 small fish cakes, flattening tops and sides with a palette knife.

8   Make a bed of sesame seeds on a plate and use them to coat fish cakes. Press seeds onto cakes using a palette knife.

9   Heat sunflower and sesame oils together in a frying pan. Fry fish cakes until golden on all sides.

10 Reheat sauce, add cream and boil to reduce slightly and concentrate flavours. Pass sauce through a sieve into a clean pan. Add lime zest, shredded blanched ginger, remaining lime leaf and seasonings. Cook briefly to blend flavours.

11 Drain fishcakes on absorbent kitchen paper. Drop lime segments into sauce, check seasonings and serve with fishcakes.

tomato tortellini

A fresh pasta dish with gutsy flavours served with Red Pesto Sauce. We are very nationalistic here and prefer to use British goats' cheese. A Welsh Pantys Gawn or a Roubiliac from Gedi in Hertfordshire are ideal. Serve with Raddichio & Rocket Salad (page 32).

SERVES 4 AS A STARTER OR
2 AS A MAIN COURSE

RED PESTO SAUCE:
1 small red pepper
4 ripe tomatoes
60 g (2 oz) sun-dried tomatoes
15 g (½ oz) pine kernels
30 g (1 oz) basil leaves
16 tablespoons good extra virgin olive oil
1 teaspoon sugar
1 fat clove garlic
salt and ground black pepper

TORTELLINI:
Fresh Saffron Pasta made with 280 g (10 oz) flour (see page 147)

FILLING:
½ small onion
2 fat cloves garlic
1 tablespoon extra virgin olive oil
12 halves sun dried tomatoes
185 g (6 oz) soft, crumbly goats' cheese
1 tablespoon chopped fresh chives

1 Prepare pesto. Roast and skin pepper (see below). Cut pepper in half and remove core and seeds. Set aside 60 g (2 oz) of pepper flesh for this sauce. Use remainder in salads. Skin fresh tomatoes (see page 48). Cut in half and scoop out seeds.

2 Toast pine kernels until golden under a hot grill or in a hot, dry frying pan. Allow to cool.

3 Purée all sauce ingredients together in a liquidiser or food processor. Season to taste with salt and pepper.

4 Prepare pasta as described on page 147 and leave to rest.

5 Prepare filling. Skin sun dried tomatoes (see below). Finely chop onion half and crush 1 clove garlic. Heat oil in a medium pan and cook onion and garlic until soft. Remove from heat and allow to cool.

6 Crumble cheese into pan with chopped chives. Chop tomatoes and stir into mixture, then season to taste – goats' cheese is usually quite salty.

7 Roll out pasta dough very thinly, or use a pasta machine on setting 6. Stamp out 12 circles using a large plain tart cutter about 10 cm (4 inch) in diameter.

8 Place a little filling on one half of each of pasta circle and dampen edges with water. Fold over and seal into semi-circular shapes. Take both ends and wrap right over left, pulling right longer than left. Fold right over left side, twist and turn ends underneath to form a little hat shape. Sit each tortellini squarely on twisted ends and chill before use.

9 Warm pesto. Boil a large pan of salted water. Add tortellini and cook for just 2 or 3 minutes – they should be 'al dente' ie. have a slight bite.

10 Drain tortellini and serve with red pesto sauce spooned over.

To skin peppers, smear with oil and roast in a very hot oven 230C (450F/Gas 8), or under a very hot grill, until the skins blister and begin to blacken. Place peppers in a polythene bag and seal. Leave for 30 minutes. The steam produced will lift the skin from the flesh. Remove peppers and peel away skin.

To skin sun dried tomatoes, cover with boiling water and leave for 10 minutes. Drain, rinse under cold water and peel away skins.

raddichio AND rocket salad

WITH HAZELNUT DRESSING

1 tablespoon hazelnuts
2 leaves raddichio
4 good handfuls rocket
1 bunch watercress
3 or 4 very white button mushrooms
2 tablespoons hazelnut oil
2 teaspoons balsamic vinegar
1 clove garlic
salt
lemon juice

*This salad makes a perfect accompaniment to Goats' Cheese &
Sun dried Tomato Tortellini (page 30).*

1 Roast hazelnuts in a hot oven at 200C (400F/Gas 6) for a few minutes until they are golden and skins come off easily. Rub off skins with a clean cloth.

2 Tear raddichio into small pieces. Wash and trim rocket and watercress. Slice mushrooms thinly. Arrange salad centrally on serving plates, adding the hazelnuts. Make a dressing by mixing together oil and vinegar. Crush a piece of garlic – not whole clove – and add to oil with salt and a little lemon juice.

3 Dress salad and serve.

mixed braised beans WITH

SWEET GARLIC CLOVES

SERVES 4

225 g (8 oz) dried butter beans
3 bulbs garlic
300 ml (10 fl oz) milk
2 beefsteak tomatoes
225 g (8 oz) fine French beans
1 kg (2 lb 4 oz) new season's broad beans
150 ml (5 fl oz) lamb stock (page 141)
1 sprig rosemary
salt and ground black pepper

*We serve this at The Old Vicarage with Pot Roasted Leg of Lamb
(page 34).*

1 Soak dried butter beans overnight and cook them as described on packet. Leave beans a little undercooked. Drain and cool. Remove skins – a tedious but simple job.

2 Remove about 16 good sized cloves garlic from bulbs. Peel cloves but leave whole.

3 Place garlic in a small pan and cover with a little cold milk. Bring to boil, drain and discard milk. Repeat twice but reserve final quantity of garlic milk.

4 Skin tomatoes (see page 48). Cut in half, remove cores and scoop out seeds with a teaspoon. Chop tomato flesh.

5 Top and tail French beans. Pod broad beans, to give 250 g (8 oz).

6 Place butter beans in a saucepan with lamb stock and rosemary. Add French beans and broad beans. Simmer until beans are just cooked but not mushy. Shake pan rather than stirring beans. When sufficiently cooked the fresh beans will be bright in colour.

7 Add tomatoes, blanched garlic and garlic milk. Remove rosemary sprig. Heat through and season to taste. Serve with sliced roast lamb, laying slices on a bed of braised beans.

creamy seafood risotto WITH

MUSHROOMS & FENNEL FRONDS

24 mussels
24 Venus clams, or fresh cockles
300 ml (10 fl oz) fish stock
150 ml (5 fl oz) water
150 ml (5 fl oz) white wine
24 uncooked shrimps, or Dublin Bay prawns
1 small onion
1 clove garlic
3 tablespoons extra virgin olive oil
60 g (2 oz) mushrooms
180 g (6 oz) arborio or risotto rice
2 teaspoons lemon juice
salt and ground black pepper
extra virgin olive oil
1 tablespoon chopped fresh parsley
1 tablespoon chopped fresh fennel leaf

A classic risotto is made with arborio rice; short, plump grains which cook to a rich creamy texture – very sophisticated yet comforting at the same time. Risotto is a dish you need to stand with and gently shake the pan during cooking to get a perfect result. Take care with the seasoning – remember the shellfish will give off sea salt.

I prefer to cook the dish in two stages, the mussels and clams first and then the risotto. It's not the classic way, but at least you can sieve the cooking liquor well and make sure that no grit gets into the rice.

1 Wash and de-beard mussels, clams or cockles.

2 Bring water and wine to boil in a wide based pan and tip in mussels and clams or cockles. Shake over a high heat for a matter of seconds until shells open. Remove shellfish with a slotted spoon.

3 Take meat from shells and set to one side. Pass cooking liquor through a fine sieve into a bowl to remove any grit. Add it to fish stock.

4 Wash and peel prawns.

5 Finely chop onion and crush garlic. Heat oil in a large frying pan and cook onion and garlic until softened.

6 Slice mushrooms thinly and add to pan with rice. Cook and stir until rice is coated with oil.

7 Add fish stock and lemon juice and bring to boil. Reduce heat to simmer and gently cook rice. Season lightly with salt and pepper.

8 Keep shaking pan and adding shellfish liquor as required. Risotto should not be dry or stick to pan but be moist and creamy.

9 Heat a little olive oil in a separate pan and stir-fry prawns until they turn pink.

10 Add cooked clams and mussels to rice and heat through. Stir in prawns and most of chopped fresh herbs, sprinkling remainder over risotto just before serving.

The whole cooking time for the rice should be about 20 minutes. Keep testing the rice – it should not be mushy. The grains should be firm without any hard, white bits in the middle. When the risotto is cooked the liquid will have been almost absorbed with a creamy residue surrounding the rice.

Shavings of Parmesan cheese, pared with a potato peeler, give an excellent finish to this risotto.

POT ROASTED leg of lamb WITH MINT &

SPRING ONION

SERVES 4

4 or 5 spring onions
1 leg of lamb, boned and rolled
salt
fresh mint
ground black pepper
30 g (1 oz) unsalted butter
1 onion
1 carrot
1 leek
1 stick celery
half a bottle light red wine
1 bay leaf

For this dish you will need a medium sized leg of lamb, about 2 kg (4 lb) in weight. Ask your butcher to bone and roll the joint for you, tying it up for roasting. Ask for the bones and trimmings for stock.

1 Preheat oven to 200C (400F/Gas 6). Lightly salt lamb bones and trimmings and place in a roasting tin. Roast in preheated oven for about 20 minutes, until browned.

2 Trim spring onions and cut into short lengths. Make incisions in lamb with a small, sharp knife and insert tiny sprigs of mint and spring onion in each incision. Season lamb with salt and pepper.

3 Heat half butter in a heavy pan or skillet and seal lamb on all sides.

4 Wash all vegetables but leave skins on (the natural dye in vegetable skins will darken and colour cooking liquor). Chop roughly.

5 Melt remaining butter in a pan, add vegetables and brown. Gradually add red wine and bring to boil. Add bay leaf and season lightly. Pour vegetables and wine into roasting tin with browned bones.

6 Sit lamb on top of vegetables and return to oven for 40 minutes. Baste occasionally during cooking. To test lamb, insert a skewer into thickest part of meat and hold it there for a count of 10. Hold skewer to your lower lip. If it is hot, lamb is cooked. Remove from oven and rest in a warm place while preparing sauce.

7 Make a sauce with lamb bones, some freshly chopped vegetables and cooking liquor, see page 92.

8 Slice lamb – it should have a pink middle and be very tender. Serve on a bed of Braised Beans with Sweet Garlic Cloves (page 32), with sauce served separately.

Spring lamb is very tender and needs shorter cooking than the bigger lambs that came later in the season. I allow 10 minutes for every 500 g (1 lb) and serve it pink. Increase this to 15 minutes for every 500 g (1 lb) for older lamb or if you prefer your meat more cooked. No longer though or the meat will not be moist and tender.

RHUBARB AND SWEET CICELY strudel WITH

RHUBARB SAUCE

SERVES 6

225 g (8 oz) caster sugar
300 ml (10 fl oz) water
1 lemon
1.4 kg (3 lb) rhubarb
2 stems sweet cicely
60 g (2 oz) unsalted butter
400 g (14 oz) packet filo pastry
(defrosted)
icing sugar, to dredge leaves or
flowers of sweet cicely, to
decorate

The best colour and freshest flavour is achieved with freshly picked young stems of forced rhubarb. An alternative to using sweet cicely would be to add a little ground star anise to the sugar syrup.

1   Place sugar and water in a saucepan and heat slowly until dissolved. Pare rind from lemon and add to pan. When sugar is dissolved, increase heat and bring to boil. Boil for 10 minutes until reduced and a heavy syrup is formed. Remove from heat.

2   Top and tail rhubarb. Cut into 5 cm (2 inch) lengths – if rhubarb is young, leave pink skins on. Remove older skins which may be tough. Add rhubarb and sweet cicely to sugar syrup, pour into a non-metallic bowl and leave to cool.

3   Preheat oven to 220C (425F/Gas 7).

4   Remove rhubarb from syrup using a slotted spoon. Pat dry with absorbent kitchen paper. Save syrup.

5   Melt butter. Lay one sheet of filo on work surface and brush with melted butter. Cut sheet in half lengthwise. Sprinkle one piece with icing sugar, then top with remaining piece. Dredge with sugar again. Turn pastry with short side towards you.

6   Place some rhubarb on pastry, about 4 cm (1½ inches) from base and fold pastry up to cover rhubarb. Fold sides edges in over fruit, then roll up to form a spring roll shape. Place on a baking sheet. Repeat to make six strudels.

7   Brush strudels with remaining butter and dredge with icing sugar. Bake in preheated oven for 12 minutes, until crisp.

8   To serve, cut ends off strudels obliquely to show filling. Serve with rhubarb syrup and decorate with small leaves or flowers of sweet cicely.

WICKED DARK chocolate tart

SERVES 6

SHORTCAKE:
250 g (8 oz) unsalted butter
125 g (4 oz) vanilla sugar
250 g (8 oz) plain flour
125 g (4 oz) semolina

CHOCOLATE FILLING:
180 g (6 oz) dark bitter chocolate
5 tablespoons cognac
4 eggs
3 tablespoons cornflour
400 g (14 oz) caster sugar
600 ml (1 pint) single cream
1 vanilla pod
125 g (4 oz) unsalted butter

*Wicked Dark Chocolate Tart has a
high gloss on the filling. It needs no
extra decoration.*

*Always buy the best chocolate you can
find – by that I mean one with a high
cocoa butter content, at least 50% if
possible. We use Valrhona which has
70% cocoa solids. Chocolat Meunier
is good and is sold in most
supermarkets.*

*I developed this dessert after eating John Tovey's gorgeous
Kentucky Chocolate Pie. My recipe uses bitter chocolate and cognac.
The method sounds involved but please persevere – it really does
work! Have the butter at room temperature before you start.*

1 Prepare the shortcake. Cream butter and vanilla sugar in a bowl until light and fluffy.

2 Mix together flour and semolina. Gradually add to butter until a crumbly dough is formed.

3 Carefully and gently knead dough until it binds together and surface is smooth.

4 Roll out lightly to line a 20 cm (8 inch) flan tin, making a base and sides as for a pastry case. Chill for 1 hour. Preheat oven to 150C (300F/Gas 2).

5 Carefully line pastry case with greaseproof paper and fill with baking beans. Bake for 20 minutes. Remove paper and beans and allow shortbread case to cool completely before filling.

6 Prepare chocolate filling. Break chocolate into squares. Place in a bowl over a pan of water or a double boiler. Add cognac to chocolate. Heat gently until chocolate is melted.

7 Beat eggs in a bowl. Blend in cornflour and sugar and add a little cream, if necessary.

8 Heat remaining cream in a saucepan with vanilla pod until almost boiling. Stir hot cream into blended egg mixture.

9 Rinse cream pan in cold water. Return mixture to pan and add melted chocolate.

10 Cook gently, stirring constantly, until mixture thickens and cornflour is cooked out – taste mixture to check it is not floury. This will take between 6 and 8 minutes. Remove vanilla pod.

11 Cool filling slightly. Soften butter and allow to cool. Beat softened butter into chocolate filling.

12 Pour into cold shortcake tart case and leave for 2 hours to set.

TOP
Wicked dark chocolate tart

LEFT
Caramelised lemon tart

RIGHT
Hazelnut meringue with crushed caramel cream

hazelnut meringue WITH

CRUSHED CARAMEL CREAM

SERVES 6

MERINGUE:
180 g (6 oz) hazelnuts
cornflour, for dusting
6 egg whites
pinch of salt
420g (15 oz) caster sugar
1½ teaspoons lemon juice
½ teaspoon natural vanilla essence
2 tablespoons strong black coffee

FILLING:
125g (4oz) caster sugar
250 g (8 oz) strawberries
150 ml (5 fl oz) double cream

This nut flavoured meringue has a lovely chewy centre! It would be equally good with a cognac flavoured cream.

1 Prepare meringue. Roast hazelnuts in a hot oven at 200C (400F/Gas 6) for a few minutes until they are golden and skins come off easily. Rub off skins with a clean cloth. Grind finely in a blender or food processor.

2 Turn oven down to 150C (300F/Gas 2). Line baking sheets with foil and dust with cornflour.

3 Whisk egg whites with a pinch of salt in a large bowl until stiff. Gradually whisk in 220 g (8 oz) sugar until stiff, glossy peaks are formed. Fold in a further 200 g (7 oz) sugar then whisk again, back to stiff peaks.

4 Using a balloon whisk, quickly and lightly fold in lemon juice, vanilla essence, black coffee and ground hazelnuts.

5 Spoon the mixture into a forcing bag fitted with a large star tube, and pipe into two circles, about 20 cm (8 inches) in diameter and 2.5 cm (1 inch) thick, on the prepared baking sheets. Speed is important before oil from nuts causes meringue to collapse.

6 Bake in preheated oven for about 45-60 minutes, until firm on outside. Cool on a wire trays, still on foil base. Peel foil away when meringue is quite cold.

7 Prepare filling. Use 125 g (4 oz) sugar and 4 tablespoons water to make a caramel (page 154). Dip strawberries – hold stalks with tweezers and dip fruits into caramel. Leave to set on silicone paper.

8 Pour remaining caramel onto a baking sheet and leave to set. When cold and brittle, place caramel between two sheets of silicone paper and crush roughly with a rolling pin.

9 Whisk cream to stiff peaks. Fold in crushed caramel.

10 Place meringue on a serving platter and top with caramel cream. Top with dipped strawberries.

For an extra treat serve this meringue with Bitter Chocolate Sauce (page 132).

CARAMELISED lemon tart

**250 g (9 oz) Old Vic shortcrust
pastry; made up weight (page 152)
1 egg white, for brushing**

FILLING:
**6 free range eggs
340 g (12 oz) caster sugar
6 lemons
320 ml (12 fl oz) double cream
icing sugar, for dredging**

*This very simple dessert has a velvety custard with a clear, zingy
flavour and melt-in-the-mouth pastry. To serve anything, other than
a scoop of vanilla ice cream with this, would simply be to gild the lily.*

1   Preheat oven to 190C (375F/Gas 5).

2   Roll out pastry on a lightly floured surface and use to line an 18 cm (7 inch) deep fluted flan tin. Bake blind (see page 105). Reduce oven temperature to 140C (275F/Gas 1).

3   Brush inside of pastry case with beaten egg white whilst it is still warm. Allow to cool completely. This will seal pastry and keep it crisp when filled.

4   Prepare filling. Whisk together eggs and sugar in a bowl until blended. Grate zests from lemons and squeeze juice. Add both to egg mixture, straining lemon juice through a fine sieve. Lightly whisk cream and fold into lemon mixture. Chill for 30 minutes.

5   Pour lemon mixture into pastry case, filling right to top of crust. Bake in centre of preheated oven for 60–75 minutes, until custard is just about set. It will still be slightly wobbly and will continue to set as it cools.

6   Allow to cool completely on a wire rack.

7   Transfer Lemon Tart to a flat serving platter and dredge thickly with icing sugar. Using a blow torch as described on page 136, apply direct heat to sugar until it melts and caramelises to a dark golden crust. When cold, this will be a crispy caramel. The same effect may be achieved by caramelising under a preheated grill, but protect pastry from burning with foil as the heat is not so concentrated and directed.

*You need a deep pastry case to make
this tart successful. Put in sufficient
baking beans when cooking the pastry
to come well up the sides, thus
preventing the pastry from shrinking
back in the tin.*

*For easier serving you may like to slice
the tart and caramelise each
individual portion as the caramel sets
hard on top. The caramel hides a very
light and delicate custard – cut
carefully with a thin, sharp knife
inserting the point first.*

summer

Long, lazy days and carefree cooking with simplicity and freshness epitomise summer to me. Immediacy of flavour and ephemeral combinations rule the day and a light touch with the cooking methods and saucing is mandatory.

With summer weather, we look to the warmer countries of the Mediterranean, North Africa, the Middle East and the Pacific Rim areas for inspirations with flavourings and ingredients.

Now is the time of outdoor eating and char-roasted vegetables. The quantity and variety of soft berry fruits available is so good it's difficult to know what to choose and the lusciousness of all the ripe stoned fruit is almost overwhelming.

ravioli OF RICOTTA, APRICOTS & CARDAMOM

SERVES 4 AS A STARTER

**Fresh Saffron Pasta made with
280 g (10 oz) flour (see page 147)
6 spring onions
1 small red pepper
60 g (2 oz) no-soak dried apricots
12 green cardamoms
1 lemon
1 tablespoon chopped fresh
chives
390 g (14 oz) ricotta cheese
salt and ground black pepper**

This ravioli recipe has a distinctly Moroccan flavour, so I serve it with a Mint Pesto (see the recipe below). The result is very fresh and unusual – I think you will like it. Make the pesto while the pasta is resting or drying.

1 Make pasta and put to rest.

2 Prepare filling. Trim and slice spring onions. Dice one quarter of red pepper. Finely chop apricots.

3 Crush cardamoms and remove seeds. Crush seeds.

4 Grate zest from lemon. Mix spring onions, red pepper, apricots, cardamom seeds, lemon zest, fresh chives and ricotta. Season to taste.

5 Divide pasta dough into 4. Roll out thinly, or use a pasta roller set at No. 6. Using a 6.5cm (2½ inch) plain tart cutter, cut out 10 circles per person.

6 Place half a teaspoonful of filling in centre of half pasta circles. Moisten edges with water and top with a second circle of pasta, firmly sealing edges together.

7 Repeat process to give 5 ravioli per person.

8 Stretch some plastic wrap over a baking sheet and dust lightly with flour. Allow ravioli to dry on baking sheet for 30 minutes.

9 Boil a large pan of salted water. Add ravioli and boil for about 2 minutes. The pasta should be 'al dente' – have a slight bite. Drain well.

10 Serve immediately with gently warmed Mint Pesto (page 56) poured over.

mint pesto

SERVES 4

PESTO:
**2 cloves garlic
4 good bunches mint
30 g (1 oz) pine kernels
½ teaspoon sugar
1 tablespoon white wine vinegar
150 ml (5 fl oz) extra virgin olive oil
Salt and freshly ground black pepper**

When we think of pesto we immediately call to mind the sweet, pungent Italian sauce for pasta. However, like all good ideas, it can be adapted. This one has the intense flavor of freshly pickled mint.

1 Prepare pesto. Peel garlic. Strip mint leaves from stems. Purée all ingredients together in a blender or food processor until smooth. Season with salt and pepper to taste.

red pepper mousse WITH

ASPARAGUS TIPS & FETA

SERVES 4

PEPPER MOUSSE:
1 small onion
1 clove garlic
15 g (½ oz) butter
1 large red pepper
300 ml (10 fl oz) double cream
salt and ground black pepper
4 sprigs tarragon
1 egg

ASPARAGUS AND FETA:
20 young asparagus spears
pinch sugar
knob of butter
iced water
90 g (3 oz) feta cheese
½ small yellow pepper
6 black olives

DRESSING:
1 tablespoon walnut oil
1 dessertspoon extra virgin olive oil
1 teaspoon balsamic vinegar
¼ level teaspoon caster sugar
salt and ground black pepper

These mousses are baked in a water bath (bain marie) to slow down the cooking. This prevents the texture from becoming grainy and ensures a velvety smooth result. There is very little egg in this recipe which is why it needs long slow cooking to gently set.

1 Prepare mousse. Preheat oven to 140C (275F/Gas 1). Lightly butter 4 dariole moulds or small ramekins.

2 Peel and finely chop onion. Peel and crush garlic. Melt butter in a small pan, add onion and garlic and cook until soft but not brown.

3 Cut red pepper in half. Remove core, seeds and membrane – you need 250 g (8 oz) prepared weight. Chop pepper roughly. Add pepper to onion with cream. Cook until vegetables are soft. Season to taste.

4 Purée in a blender or food processor. Rinse saucepan. Pass mixture through a fine sieve into clean pan.

5 Strip leaves from tarragon and chop finely. Beat egg. Heat mixture gently. Add tarragon and beaten egg off the heat.

6 Pour into prepared moulds and cover each one with foil. Place two folded muslins or household cloths in a roasting tin. Sit moulds on cloths. Pour sufficient boiling water into tin to come one quarter of way up moulds.

7 Bake in preheated oven for 1–1¼ hours, until mousses are set. Leave to cool.

8 Prepare asparagus. Remove woody white ends of spears. Cut away stems, leaving just tips and about 5 cm (2 inches) of stem. Use trimmings to make soup or to purée into a sauce. Bring a small pan of water to boiling point. Add asparagus tips, a pinch of sugar and a knob of butter. Cook for about 2 minutes, until just cooked but still crisp. Drain and refresh in iced water. Drain again.

9 Cut feta cheese into very small dice. Remove core, seeds and membrane from yellow pepper. Cut flesh into very small dice. Stone olives, cut each one into six pieces and mix with cheese and yellow pepper in a small bowl.

10 Prepare dressing. Whisk oils, vinegar and sugar together in a bowl or small jug. Season to taste with salt and pepper.

11 Run a small sharp knife around mousses. Invert onto four serving plates, give a sharp shake to remove mousses from tins. Arrange asparagus around mousses, like spokes of a wheel. Place teaspoonfuls of feta mixture between asparagus spears. Drizzle dressing over asparagus and cheese immediately before serving.

gazpacho

SERVES 4

½ **small onion**
2 cloves garlic
6 tablespoons extra virgin olive oil
8 ripe tomatoes
1 small cucumber
2 red peppers
bunch fresh basil
1 yellow pepper
**600 ml (1 pint) white chicken
stock**
½ **tablespoon tomato purée**
dash Tabasco
1 tablespoon white wine vinegar
½ **teaspoon caster sugar**
salt and ground black pepper
chopped fresh chives

RIGHT
Gazpacho

BELOW
*Hazelnut toasted goats' cheese with
tomato bruschetta and Smoked pepper
salsa*

*This chilled soup is simplicity itself to make. Prepare it several
hours before required so that it may be well chilled in the refrigerator.*

*Serve on hot, sultry days accompanied by a dish of plump black
olives and glasses of chilled old oloroso or amontillado sherry to evoke
memories of the cool, white courtyards and olive groves of Andalucia.*

1   Peel and finely chop small onion half. Peel and crush garlic. Heat 1
    tablespoon olive oil in a pan, add onion and garlic, cover and cook
    gently until soft. This will take out any raw, bitter flavours. Cool.

2   Reserve vegetables for garnish – one tomato, one quarter of
    cucumber, a small piece red pepper and some basil.

3   Wash and roughly chop all remaining vegetables, leaving skins on for
    added flavour and colour.

4   Purée chopped vegetables, remaining oil, chicken stock, tomato
    puree, Tabasco, vinegar and sugar together in a blender or food
    processor until smooth. Pass through a fine sieve and season to taste
    with salt and pepper.

5   Chill in the refrigerator for at least two hours.

6   Prepare with vegetable garnish. Halve tomato and scoop out seeds
    with a teaspoon. Finely dice tomato, cucumber and pepper and shred
    basil. Sprinkle over soup with chives.

HAZELNUT TOASTED goats' cheese WITH TOMATO BRUSCHETTA

SERVES 4

4 thick slices Ciabatta Italian bread
1 clove garlic
2 × 125 g (4 oz) goats' cheeses (see notes on goats' cheese, page 30)
225 g (8 oz) roasted hazelnuts (see page 152)
2 tablespoons hazelnut oil
4 plum tomatoes
6 spring onions
4 halves sun dried tomatoes
4 anchovy fillets
4 black olives
6 leaves basil
extra virgin olive oil

Use a soft, crumbly, rindless goat's cheese for this dish. You could, if you wish, marinate the cheese for a few days in olive oil with a sprig of rosemary. This is an excellent idea if the cheese is rather mild in flavour. If you do marinate the cheese, make certain that you drain it well on absorbent kitchen paper before coating it with the hazelnuts. The cheese melts slightly during grilling. You will notice that it develops a totally different character and flavour.

We serve a Smoked Pepper Salsa (page 151) to accompany this at the Old Vicarage.

1 Preheat oven to 140C (275F/Gas 1).

2 Cut four slices of Ciabatta diagonally from loaf. Rub bread with olive oil. Cut garlic in half, then rub cut surface over bread. Place on a baking sheet and dry in oven until very crisp about 15–20 minutes.

3 Divide cheeses in half and reshape into rounds. Chop hazelnuts very finely. Coat cheese in nuts, pressing them into surface. Set on a plate and drizzle with hazelnut oil. Chill until required.

4 Skin tomatoes (see below). Trim spring onions, then slice tomatoes and onions. Skin sun-dried tomatoes (see page 30) and split anchovy fillets in half. Stone olives and cut in half.

5 Shred basil leaves finely and scatter over crisp bread. Top with spring onions, plum and sun dried tomatoes, anchovies and olives. Scatter these freely over the bruschetta – this is a rough, country dish. Drizzle olive oil over.

6 Bruschetta need fierce heat to gain a charred appearance without tomatoes becoming mushy. Use a very hot grill or a very hot oven. Toast bruschetta quickly until just starting to blacken.

7 Toast goat's cheese under a preheated grill until browned and crisp on outside and just beginning to melt inside. Serve immediately with tomato bruschetta.

To skin tomatoes, peaches and plums. Place your fruit in a bowl, cover with boiling water and leave for no more than 30 seconds. Remove fruit with a slotted spoon and plunge into iced water to cool rapidly. Lift the skin with the knife from the flower (not the stalk) end – it will slide off easily

The bruschetta may be blackened with a blowtorch (see page 36).

You may like to spread a little pesto over the sliced bread instead of using shredded basil.

roast leg of lamb WITH FRESH

CHERRY & SPEARMINT COMPOTE

2.3 kg (5 lb) leg of lamb, boned
2 fat cloves garlic
few sprigs fresh spearmint
30 g (1 oz) softened unsalted
butter
salt and ground black pepper

CHERRY AND SPEARMINT COMPOTE:
a good handful spearmint
½ teaspoon sugar
2 tablespoons crab apple jelly (see
recipe p 149) or use rowan jelly or
redcurrant jelly
squeeze of fresh lemon juice
450 g (1 lb) cherries

Choose a leg of lamb about 2.5 kg (5 lb) in weight. Ask your butcher to bone it out for you, trimming off excess fat and tying the joint ready for roasting. Ask him also to return the bones for stock.

The meat may be cooked on the bone if preferred. Increase roasting time to 1 hour (with 10 minutes resting time) for pink meat.

1 Preheat oven to 220C (425F/Gas 7).

2 Make small incisions all over lamb with tip of a sharp knife. Peel garlic and cut into slivers. Insert into incisions with spearmint leaves.

3 Rub lamb with a little softened butter. Season lightly.

4 Heat a griddle or a large skillet until evenly hot (see page 53). Sear meat on all sides to seal.

5 Transfer lamb to a roasting tin. Roast in preheated oven for 50 minutes, turning lamb over once during cooking.

6 Prepare Cherry and Spearmint Compôte while lamb is cooking. Strip leaves from a good handful of spearmint. Place on a chopping board and scatter with sugar. Chop finely.

7 Heat crab apple jelly in a small pan. Add chopped mint and continue to heat until jelly has melted and there are no lumps.

8 Add a squeeze of lemon juice if necessary to enliven flavours. Remove pan from heat. Stone and add cherries. The heat from jelly will be quite enough to soften cherries without allowing them to cook down to a pulp. Cool and chill lightly before serving.

9 Test lamb by inserting a skewer into thickest part of meat and holding it there for a count of 10. Touch skewer to your lips – if it feels hot meat is cooked. (As season progresses I find that lamb progressively needs a little longer, 5 minutes or so, to cook to same degree.) Transfer lamb to a warming oven for 10 minutes before carving.

10 Carve lamb and serve overlapping slices with Cherry & Spearmint Compôte served separately.

Serve with fresh vegetables in season. I would suggest new potatoes, and fresh peas and broad beans. I cook broad beans and slip off their skins to reveal the bright green beans. Then I cook fresh peas in a little butter with a hearty cos lettuce, shredded finely, just for 2 or 3 minutes. Add the shelled beans with a little double cream. Season and add a tablespoon of chopped fresh parsley.

LAVENDER ROASTED poussins WITH PINE KERNELS & MADEIRA

SERVES 4 AS A STARTER OR 2 AS A MAIN COURSE

2 oven-ready poussins
60 g (2 oz) softened butter
salt and ground black pepper
4 spring onions
16 sprigs lavender
30 g (1 oz) pine kernels

SAUCE:
1 small onion
1 small carrot
1 stick celery
90 g (3 oz) chilled unsalted butter
150 ml (5 fl oz) red wine
150 ml (5 fl oz) Madeira
150 ml (5 fl oz) reduced chicken stock (page 141)
4 juniper berries

We usually think of lavender in terms of scent and pot pouris. As a culinary flavouring it is somewhat akin to thyme but with a spicier flavour – give it a try – you will be pleasantly surprised!

1   Preheat oven to 220C (425F/Gas 7).

2   Remove any stray feathers or quills from poussins. Wash and pat dry.

3   Loosen skin over breast bones and work half softened butter over meat under skin. Season poussins inside and out.

4   Trim and chop spring onions. Mix with half lavender. Divide between poussin cavities.

5   Melt remaining softened butter in a skillet and seal birds on breasts. Turn until browned and sealed all over.

6   Strew remaining lavender in a roasting tin and sit poussins on top, breasts down. This keeps meat moist during cooking. Roast in preheated oven for 5 minutes. Turn birds, add pine kernels and roast for a further 3 minutes.

7   Remove poussins from oven. Cut off whole breasts and remove legs and thighs together from carcasses.

8   Loosely cover breasts (which will be pink) with foil and keep them warm. Return legs and thighs to oven for a further 2 minutes. Keep warm with poussin breasts.

9   Make sauce. Use half onion and carrot. Peel and chop finely. Chop celery.

10 Fry vegetables until golden in juices in meat tin with a knob of butter over a medium heat. Add red wine, bring to boil and reduce over a high heat to a sticky glaze. Scrape up any meat sediment in pan into glaze.

11 Add Madeira and reduce again. Break up poussin carcasses and add to tin with chicken stock and juniper. Reduce again.

12 Pass sauce through a fine sieve into a clean pan. Whisk in sufficient of remaining chilled butter, a little at a time, to make a light, glossy coating sauce. Season to taste.

13 If serving with polenta cakes, place one on each plate and prop a poussin leg up against it. Slice poussin breasts and overlap slices. Spoon sauce around plate. Garnish with lavender sprigs and flowers.

We serve this at the Old Vicarage with Polenta Cakes (page 146), allowing one per person.

fillet of wild salmon STEAMED

WITH ELDERFLOWERS & MUSCAT SAUCE

SERVES 4

750 g (1½ lb) fillet of wild salmon
salt and ground black pepper
1 leek
half a bottle of Muscat d'Alsace
150 g (5 oz) chilled unsalted
butter
6 heads of elderflowers
1 small onion
150 ml (5 fl oz) fish stock (see
page 140)

TO SERVE:
1 kg (2 lb 4 oz) asparagus
450 g (1 lb) fresh samphire
30 g (1 oz) unsalted butter
chopped fresh chives

Elderflowers and samphire both grow wild in early summer and make a lovely combination with wild salmon. The elderflowers impart a heady muscat flavour to the fish, enhanced by the sauce and balanced by the fresh salty tanginess of the samphire. Photographed on the cover.

1   Preheat oven to 200C (400F/Gas 6).

2   Skin and bone salmon fillet. Remove any dark meat from skin side of fillet. Cut into four pieces and season lightly.

3   Cut four pieces of foil, large enough to loosely enclose salmon.

4   Finely shred white part only of leek and divide between four pieces of foil. Moisten each pile with a tablespoon of wine. Add a knob of butter and a little seasoning.

5   Wash elderflower heads in running water. Sit salmon on leeks and top each piece with a head of elderflowers.

6   Lift opposite edges of foil together to centre of parcel, folding over to seal loosely into parcels.

7   Place foil packets on a baking sheet. Bake in preheated oven for 4–6 minutes, depending on thickness of fish. Remove salmon from oven and leave in sealed packets for another 2 minutes.

8   Prepare sauce while salmon is baking. Peel and finely chop onion. Melt a little butter in a saucepan, add onion and cook until soft.

9   Add fish stock, remaining wine and 1 head of elderflowers. Bring to boiling point, then boil until reduced by half. Taste. Continue reducing sauce until the flavour is to your liking.

10 Strain sauce through a fine sieve into a clean pan. Whisk in remaining chilled butter to give a thickened, glossy sauce. Season to taste.

11 Prepare asparagus and cook briefly in boiling salted water for between 30 seconds and 2 minutes, depending on thickness of stems. It should be tender but crisp. Drain. Wash samphire. Stir fry in butter for a few seconds, then add chives.

12 Pile samphire onto serving plates and arrange asparagus to the side. Unwrap foil packets and discard elderflowers. Place the salmon on the samphire and pour the sauce round. Scatter a few flowers from the remaining head of elderflowers over the salmon immediately before serving.

Samphire can be freely picked around coastal areas, either clinging to the sea walls (rock samphire) or growing in salt marshes (marsh samphire). It can also be ordered from your fishmonger in the early summer months. It is crisp and salty and tastes a bit like asparagus.

GRIDDLED fillet of angus beef

WITH THYME & MUSHROOMS

SERVES 4

1 kg (2 lb 4 oz) piece fillet of beef
8 sprigs thyme
1 tablespoon extra virgin olive oil
salt and ground black pepper

SAUCE:
1 glass red wine
300 ml (10 fl oz) beef stock (see
page 141)
90 g (3 oz) chilled unsalted butter

SPINACH AND MUSHROOMS:
1 small clove garlic
340 g (12 oz) mushrooms
30 g (1 oz) unsalted butter
750 g (1½ lb) young spinach leaves
salt and ground black pepper
freshly grated nutmeg

This is a very simple and quick dish to prepare – it therefore follows that you must buy the very best quality prime Angus beef for it. The quality will shine through. We serve this at the Old Vicarage with Pissaladière (page 143).

1 Preheat oven to 220C (425F/Gas 7).

2 Trim fillet of loose chain of meat, any cartilage and skin. There should be no obvious fat on the outside of fillet. Set fillet to one side.

3 Cut up trimmings. Place in a small roasting tin. Brown in the preheated oven for 20 minutes or so.

4 Make incisions in beef fillet with tip of a sharp knife. Insert tiny sprigs of thyme.

5 Cut fillet into four evenly sized steaks. Rub lightly with olive oil and season with salt and pepper.

6 Prepare sauce. Pour red wine into roasting tin with beef trimmings and place on hob. Bring to boil, scraping up any sediment from pan into wine. Reduce oven to 200C (400F/Gas 6).

7 Pour beef stock into a saucepan. Add contents of roasting tin. Bring to boiling point. Simmer down to a good rich gravy.

8 Heat a griddle or cast iron frying pan until evenly hot (see below). Cook fillets top and bottom for 2 minutes each side, then sear round sides.

9 For medium to rare beef, place fillet on a baking sheet and roast in oven for 4 minutes. Rest in warming oven for a further 3 to 4 minutes.

10 Strain sauce through a sieve into a clean pan. Season to taste. Whisk in 90 g (3 oz) chilled butter, a little at a time, to finish sauce and give it a good gloss. Set to one side.

11 While fillet is cooking prepare the spinach. Peel and crush garlic. Trim and slice mushrooms. Cook in a saucepan with 15 g (½ oz) butter until mushrooms have softened. Season to taste.

12 Melt the remaining 15 g (½ oz) butter in a wide pan and add young spinach leaves. Heat until spinach just wilts. Add salt, pepper and grated nutmeg.

13 Serve beef on a bed of spinach. Make a pile of mushrooms to one side. Pour sauce over and around beef.

To test a griddle or cast iron pan for an even heat. Heat the griddle until very hot, then reduce the heat to low to maintain the temperature without overheating. Hold the flat of your hand 15cm (6 inches) above the surface of the griddle. When it feels evenly hot the griddle is ready.

If there are any large stalks in the spinach, remove them before starting to prepare the beef. Always wash spinach in plenty of cold water to remove any grittiness. Many supermarkets now sell washed young spinach leaves, but they are very expensive.

FAR RIGHT
Golden fillet of turbot with deep fried leek and mint pesto

RIGHT
Chargrilled wild salmon with lime and ginger

BELOW
Lemon grass & honey dressing

lemon grass & honey DRESSING

SERVES 4

4 sticks lemon grass
300 ml (10 fl oz) fish stock (see page 140)
2 bunches watercress
2 large limes
1 teaspoon honey (orange blossom or acacia)
1 tablespoon hazelnut oil
1 tablespoon walnut oil
salt and ground black pepper
1 tablespoon chopped fresh garlic chives, if available or use fresh chives

1 Trim and peel away outer layer of lemon grass. Place in a small pan, cover with cold water and bring to boiling point. Drain. Chop lemon grass finely.

2 Heat half fish stock until boiling. Plunge watercress into stock and remove immediately from heat. The watercress will wilt. Purée watercress and liquor in a blender or liquidiser until smooth. Pass through a fine sieve into a clean bowl. You will need 2 tablespoons for the dressing. Freeze the remainder for another day.

3 Boil remaining stock until reduced by half. Grate zests and squeeze juice from limes. Add zest and half juice to stock with honey and chopped lemon grass. Simmer for 2 or 3 minutes to blend flavours.

4 Add 2 tablespoons watercress purée, hazelnut and walnut oils. Whisk together vigorously until blended. Season to taste.

5 Add garlic chives at very last moment. Serve warm with fish.

GOLDEN fillet of turbot WITH DEEP

FRIED LEEK AND MINT PESTO

SERVES 4

MINT PESTO:
2 cloves garlic
4 good bunches mint
30 g (1 oz) pine kernels
½ teaspoon sugar
1 tablespoon white wine vinegar
150 ml (5 fl oz) extra virgin olive oil
Salt and ground black pepper

TURBOT AND LEEK:
1 leek
390 g (14 oz) fillet of turbot
2 teaspoons plain flour
salt and ground black pepper
2 tablespoons extra virgin olive oil
sunflower oil, for deep fat frying

At the Old Vicarage we make a non-purist pesto without cheese which makes a splendid accompaniment to many dishes – it allows the other flavours to shine through and works particularly well with fish. Serve with 125 g (4 oz) Fresh Pasta (page 147), made into spaghetti tagliatelli and tossed in butter and chopped fresh chives.

1 Prepare pesto. Peel garlic. Strip mint leaves from stems. Purée all ingredients together in a blender or food processor until smooth. Season with salt and pepper to taste.

2 Preheat oven to 200C (400F/Gas 6).

3 Trim leek and shred very finely. Spread out on absorbent kitchen paper and leave on top of cooker or in a warm place to dry.

4 Skin turbot and cut into four pieces. Season lightly and dust top side of fillet lightly with flour.

5 Heat a heavy based pan or cast iron skillet until it is evenly hot. Add olive oil and heat. Cook turbot, floured side down, until a crisp golden crust is formed. The fish will release easily from pan when crust is ready – don't force it as presentation will be spoiled. Remove fish from pan and place on a baking sheet, crust side uppermost.

6 Bake turbot for 4–5 minutes, until just cooked. Warm pesto gently.

7 Heat deep fryer until a cube of bread browns quickly and floats to surface of pan. Fry leek for 15 seconds, until crisp. Drain on absorbent kitchen paper.

8 Serve turbot on a bed of spaghetti or tagliatelli, topped with fried leek and with pesto sauce spooned round.

Make the pasta well in advance and allow it to dry – the tagliatelli will only take 1 minute to cook in boiling salted water. Store pesto in a screw-top jar in the refrigerator. It will keep for a week or so without losing its flavour or colour.

CHARGRILLED wild salmon WITH

LIME & GINGER

750 g (1½ lb) fillet of wild salmon
salt and ground black pepper
extra virgin olive oil
3 pieces stem ginger
1 lime
1 tablespoon extra virgin olive oil
1 tablespoon syrup from stem ginger

Chargrilled fish is best cooked outdoors on a charcoal barbecue to give it an authentic charred appearance and flavour. Chargrilled food is atmospheric – it evokes a laid-back mood – it's right for summer. We can simulate the effect inside on a griddle – and why not? We so often need to be inventive with our weather!

1 Skin the salmon and pick out as many bones as possible with tweezers. Remove any dark meat from skin side of fillet. Cut salmon into 4 even pieces, season lightly and rub with olive oil.

2 Cut stem ginger into fine matchsticks or Julienne.

3 Grate zest from half lime and mix with ginger. Spread over upper side of salmon.

1 **TO CHARGRILL SALMON:** make sure that coals have burnt down to a white hot mass with plenty of residual heat.

2 Squeeze juice from half lime and mix with olive oil and ginger syrup. Brush over salmon. This is the basting liquid.

3 Cook salmon on one side until it has a crisp charred surface. Do not attempt to move salmon until surface has carbonised otherwise the pieces will stick and the presentation will be spoiled.

4 Brush the salmon with basting liquid, turn and cook second side until crisp and golden.

5 Move fish to edge of barbecue, where it is cooler, and leave for 1 or 2 minutes. The salmon will be cooked through with a crisp coating and a soft, juicy pink inside.

TO CHARGRIDDLE THE SALMON INSIDE: you will need a cast iron skillet or a griddle with a grid effect. Failing this, heat a few metal skewers in a gas flame until red hot and sear the top surface of the salmon with bar markings.

Heat the skillet or griddle to a very hot even heat, then cook the salmon in exactly the same way as above.

We serve this with a dressing of Lemon Grass & Honey (page 54) at the Old Vicarage.

roast red mullet WITH TOMATO &

OLIVE OIL DRESSING

SERVES 4 AS A STARTER

DRESSING:
1 small onion
2 fat cloves garlic
2 tablespoons extra virgin olive oil
12 tomatoes
¼ small red pepper
1 teaspoon salt
freshly ground black pepper
handful fresh basil leaves
extra virgin olive oil
1 tablespoon wine vinegar

2 × 375 g (12 oz) red mullet
4 sprigs basil

Red mullet has a pretty pink skin and a strong, gamey flavour.

Ask your fishmonger to scale and fillet the mullet, but to leave the skin on. Double the quantities to serve 4 as a main course.

1 Prepare dressing. Peel onion and chop half finely. Peel and crush garlic. Heat oil in a pan and cook chopped onion and garlic slowly until soft but not browned.

2 Chop tomatoes roughly. Chop red pepper flesh. Add tomatoes and pepper to pan with salt and pepper and simmer to a thick sauce.

3 Purée in a blender or food processor. Pass through a fine sieve into a measuring jug.

4 Preheat oven to 200C (400F/Gas 6).

5 Mix 2 parts of sauce with one part extra virgin olive oil and 1 tablespoon wine vinegar. Whisk together until blended.

6 Scale and fillet mullet if your fishmonger has not done this for you. Season flesh and rub skins with a little olive oil. Cut each fish into two fillets down the backbone.

7 Place a few sprigs of basil in a small roasting tin and top with mullet fillets, skin side up. Roast in preheated oven for 3 or 4 minutes.

8 Reheat dressing gently in a clean saucepan before serving, whisking continuously, and scatter with torn basil leaves.

9 Serve red mullet with dressing poured round.

Serve the mullet with Tapenade (page 150) and a small quantity of Saffron Noodles, made with 125 g (4 oz) fresh pasta (page 147). Serve the mullet on a pile of noodles in the centre of a plate, with a generous teaspoon of tapenade and the dressing poured round.

summer pudding

SERVES 4

180 g (6 oz) blackcurrants
180 g (6 oz) redcurrants
180 g (6 oz) blueberries or
bilberries
180 g (6 oz) small strawberries
180 g (6 oz) raspberries
180 g (6 oz) cherries
4–6 tablespoons caster sugar
1 lemon
1 large loaf stone ground
wholemeal bread
mint leaves
icing sugar
pouring cream, to serve

The varieties of fruit used in this pudding do not matter so long as the quantities are right. Make it the day before it is needed to allow the fruit juices to permeate right through the bread. For the best finish it is important to use a close-textured wholemeal bread. Commercial white sliced bread develops a slimy texture and is quite disgusting!

1   Reserve a few attractive little bunches of berries to decorate puddings. Strip stalks and hulls from all fruits. Stone cherries.

2   Place all fruits in a pan with 4 tablespoons sugar. Pare zest from lemon in large pieces with a sharp knife and add to pan. Heat gently, only until juices flow. Remove from heat.

3   Check sweetness and add more sugar if necessary.

4   Set a colander over a bowl to collect juices. Pour fruit into colander. Remove lemon zest.

5   Trim crusts from loaf and slice quite thinly. Cut out 4 bread circles to fit bases of 4 individual pudding tins. Cut 8 rectangles of bread, each being same height as tins and half its width. Arrange bread inside tins to form a complete lining.

6   Remove bread from tins and soak it in the deep red fruit syrup. Reline tins with soaked bread, making sure that there are no gaps.

7   Pack prepared fruit into tins, filling right to top of bread.

8   Cut 4 more circles of bread to fit over puddings. Dip in fruit juices and place on top of fruit.

9   Cover puddings with plastic wrap and set on a tray. Cover with another tray. Press with heavy weights or cans of food. Chill in refrigerator overnight.

10 Purée any remaining fruit with syrup in a blender or food processor. Pass through a fine sieve into a container and chill in refrigerator.

11 Trim away any excess bread before serving. Run a small, thin bladed knife around each pudding and invert onto a serving plate. Give a good shake to remove puddings from tins. Pour a little sauce over and around each pudding, making sure that top and sides are coated and have a deep gloss.

12 Arrange reserved sprigs of berries on top and around puddings with some small mint leaves. Dust lightly with icing sugar.

13 Serve with a jug of pouring cream.

Process any remaining bread into breadcrumbs and freeze for later use.

strawberry & rose petal

SHORTCAKE

SHORTCAKE:
500 g (1lb) unsalted butter
250 g (8 oz) vanilla flavoured
caster sugar
500g (1 lb) plain flour
250 g (8 oz) semolina
caster sugar, to dredge

ROSE CREAM:
2 teaspoons lemon juice
3 large red old-fashioned scented
roses
300 ml (10 fl oz) double cream
1 tablespoon icing sugar
½ teaspoon rose water

FILLING AND DECORATION:
750 g (1½ lb) ripe strawberries
2 rose buds

The strawberries for decoration may be dipped in caramel before being placed on the shortbread (see page 38). The rose buds may be crystallised – this should be done the day before. Take the petals from the buds (or use small petals from the centre of an open rose). Leave to dry on absorbent kitchen paper. Paint dry petals with lightly beaten egg white, using a clean artists paintbrush – do not leave any blobs of egg white on the petals. Dredge with caster sugar from a fine dredger and leave on absorbent kitchen paper to dry out. The petals will become firm and crisp but retain their natural appearance.

The same technique can be used for any edible flowers such as borage, elderflowers, violets etc.

Roses are quintessentially English, like afternoon tea and strawberries and cream. Distilled rose water, however, originated in Persia over 2000 years ago and has played a special part in Middle Eastern cookery ever since.

Use dark red, fragrant roses to flavour the cream. Pick them in the morning on a dry day and examine them carefully for insects before use. Do not use roses which have been sprayed with insecticide.

This shortcake makes a lovely fragrant dessert.

1 Prepare shortcake. Cream together butter and vanilla sugar in a large bowl until light and fluffy.

2 Sieve together flour and semolina. Gradually work into creamed mixture. Use your hands to blend at end of mixing.

3 Knead on a lightly floured surface until smooth. Divide into two pieces and press into two 20 cm (8 inch) fluted flan rings on a baking sheet, or flan tins. Prick shortcakes all over with a fork and rest for 30 minutes in the refrigerator.

4 Preheat oven to 150C (300F/Gas 2).

5 Prepare rose cream. Place lemon juice in a bowl. Crush rose petals in your hand and drop into lemon juice. Turn petals over gently in juice to keep colour bright. Add cream, icing sugar and rosewater. Stir to blend. Leave for flavours to infuse for 30 minutes in a cool place.

6 Bake shortcakes in preheated oven for 25–30 minutes, until just tinged golden.

7 Mark one into 8 portions with a sharp knife while still warm. Dredge lightly with caster sugar. Allow to cool before removing from tins.

8 Assemble shortcake. Place unmarked shortcake on a serving plate.

9 Sieve cream and discard petals. Whisk until cream is firm but not stiff and dry. Taste and add a little sugar if necessary.

10 Spread half cream over shortcake base. Reserve 9 strawberries for decoration. Hull and slice remaining strawberries and arrange over cream. Top with remaining cream.

11 Finish with marked shortcake. Arrange a strawberry on each portion of shortbread and place one in centre. Garnish with rosebuds or rose petals.

raspberry pavlova WITH FRESH

RASPBERRY PUREE

4 large egg whites
pinch salt
375 g (12 oz) caster sugar
1 tablespoon granulated sugar
1 tablespoon cornflour
3 teaspoons lemon juice
600 g (1¼ lb) raspberries
300 ml (10 fl oz) double cream

Contrary to popular belief I find that near frozen egg whites whisk up to a greater volume than fresh ones. Eggs a few days old whisk up better than very fresh ones. Keep everything very cool when making meringues. This keeps the volume high and the meringue light. The combination of lemon juice, granulated sugar and cornflour gives the pavlova its characteristic crisp outside and marshmallow inside.

1 Preheat oven to 120C (250F/Gas ½). Cover an upturned baking sheet with foil.

2 Whisk egg whites with a pinch of salt until stiff. Gradually add 125 g (4 oz) caster sugar, then whisk again until egg whites are very glossy and stiff. Add a further 90 g (3 oz) caster sugar, then whisk back to glossy peaks.

3 Sieve together granulated sugar and cornflour. Use a balloon whisk to lightly fold in half cornflour mixture, then 1 teaspoon lemon juice, then remaining cornflour.

4 Place a large star tube in a forcing bag and fill with half pavlova mixture.

5 Spread remaining mixture in a circle, about 18 cm (7 inches) in diameter, on baking sheet. Smooth top and sides. Pipe swirls of meringue around top of circle. Pavlova should be about 6 cm (2½ inches) thick.

6 Bake in preheated oven for about 2–2½ hours. Do not allow meringue to colour.

7 Dissolve remaining sugar in 150 ml (5 fl oz) water in a small saucepan. Bring to boil then simmer for 10 minutes to make a heavy syrup.

8 Add 400 g (12 oz) raspberries to syrup with remaining 2 teaspoons lemon juice. Purée in a blender or food processor until smooth. Pass coulis through a fine sieve to remove seeds. Pour into a serving jug and chill.

9 Cool pavlova on the baking sheet. When cold, carefully peel off foil.

10 Whip cream until thick. Pipe swirls of cream around pavlova and top with remaining raspberries. Serve with raspberry coulis.

PREVIOUS PAGE

FAR RIGHT
Strawberry tarts with vanilla pastry cream

RIGHT
Strawberry and rose petal shortcake

LEFT
Raspberry pavlova.

strawberry tarts WITH VANILLA PASTRY CREAM

What could be better than fresh English strawberries, ripe, luscious and warm from the sun?

SERVES 4

250 g (9 oz) 'Old Vic' Foolproof Pastry (see page 152)

PASTRY CREAM:
3 egg yolks
1 tablespoon caster sugar
½ teaspoon cornflour
1½ tablespoons plain flour
430 ml (15 fl oz) single cream
2 vanilla pods
1 tablespoon strawberry liqueur

250 g (9 oz) strawberries

These tarts may be served with a warm Strawberry Soufflé.

1 Preheat oven to 200C (400F/Gas 6). Roll out pastry and use to line 4 individual 10 cm (4 inch) tart tins. Bake blind (see page 105).

2 Prepare a pastry cream. Blend egg yolks in a bowl with sugar, cornflour, flour and a little cream. Pour remaining cream into a saucepan. Split vanilla pods and add to cream. Bring to boiling point.

3 Pour boiling cream onto egg in a steady stream, whisking constantly. Rinse pan in cold water. Return custard to pan and cook over a low heat for 2 or 3 minutes, beating vigorously. It is ready when there is no residual taste of flour.

4 Remove vanilla pods. Scrape out seeds and add to custard. Stir in strawberry liqueur, cool and chill. Spoon pastry cream into tarts when cold then top with sliced strawberries.

strawberry soufflé

This dreamy light foolproof soufflé is made without a custard base, so nothing masks the flavour of the fruit. This is a warm soufflé, perfect for entertaining as it needs only 4 or 5 minutes baking.

SERVES 4

750 g (1½ lb) strawberries
180 g (6 oz) caster sugar
1 lemon
icing sugar, for dusting
unsalted butter, for greasing
caster sugar, for dusting
5 egg whites
pinch salt

These soufflés make a marvellous dessert on their own, or just with fresh strawberries. Served with Strawberry Tarts, however, the contrasting textures and visual appeals make the combination a certain winner!

1 Hull strawberries. Purée in a blender or food processor with 60 g (2 oz) caster sugar and juice of half a lemon. Pass through a fine sieve into a saucepan.

2 Boil purée until reduced to about one quarter of original volume, to a thick strawberry concentrate. Transfer to a bowl, cool then chill.

3 Preheat oven to 200C (400F/Gas 6). Lightly butter and sugar four ramekins. Place a tablespoon strawberry concentrate in each.

4 Whisk egg whites with a pinch of salt to form stiff peaks. Fold in 2 tablespoons of remaining sugar. Whisk back to stiff peaks. Whisk in remaining sugar. Use a balloon whisk to fold in concentrated strawberry purée. Pile soufflé into ramekins, allowing mixture to stand about 5cm (2 inches) above top of ramekin. Smooth tops and sides with a palette knife.

5 Bake in preheated oven for 4–5 minutes, until risen and golden. Remove from oven. Dust with icing sugar and serve immediately.

gooseberry & elderflower fool

SERVES 4

150 ml (5 fl oz) Easy Foolproof Custard (see page 68)
150 ml (5 fl oz) double cream
1 teaspoon icing sugar
6 heads elderflowers
600 g (1¼ lb) ripe gooseberries
150 ml (5 fl oz) water
340 g (12 oz) caster sugar

Elderflowers, with their pretty lacy flower caps and intoxicating Muscat scent, are everywhere in the countryside during June. Pick the ones which are furthest away from roads and check that they are insect free. Nature has contrived to have elderflowers in bloom at the same time as the gooseberries ripen. They have a wonderful affinity. Try them together in pies, ice cream or in this very simple fool. I'm sure you'll love the combination.

1   Make custard as directed on page 68. Cool and chill.

2   Whisk cream with icing sugar until firm, but not stiff and dry. Chill.

3   Wash elderflower heads under slowly running water. Place four in a saucepan with gooseberries, water and majority of sugar. Cook gently until fruit breaks down and cooks to a pulp.

4   Remove elderflower heads. Sieve fruit into a clean pan.

5   Boil fruit extract until reduced to a thick purée. Taste and add remaining sugar if necessary. Cool and chill.

6   Take tiny flowers from one of remaining heads of elderflowers and stir into chilled gooseberry purée.

7   Place alternate spoonfuls of custard, cream and fruit purée in a wide bowl. Using a spatula, draw them lightly together to make a green, yellow and white marbled fool.

8   Spoon into pretty glass dishes to show off marbled effect. Take tiny sprigs of elderflowers from remaining head. Dust with caster sugar and shake off excess, then use to decorate fools.

Serve with Almond Tuilles, page 153.

queen of puddings WITH FRESH
STRAWBERRIES & FLAKED ALMONDS

SERVES 4

600 ml (1 pint) Quick Foolproof Custard (see below)

60 g (2 oz) fresh white breadcrumbs
1 lemon
3 tablespoons strawberry jam
180 g (6 oz) strawberries

MERINGUE:
5 egg whites
5 tablespoons caster sugar
1 tablespoon flaked almonds

This is a true nursery pudding. The charm of the meringue topping is in the crisp, swirly peaks tinged with a light golden colour – it also utilises the egg whites left over from the custard.

1   Make the Foolproof Custard.

2   Sprinkle breadcrumbs and grated zest from lemon into a 1 litre (1¾ pint) ovenproof serving dish and pour the hot custard over. Cool, then chill in the refrigerator for 2 hours.

3   Preheat oven to 120C (250F/Gas ½).

4   Warm jam, either in a bowl over a saucepan of water or briefly in microwave. Spread top of custard with warm jam. Hull and slice strawberries, arrange over jam.

5   Prepare meringue. Whisk egg whites in a bowl with a pinch of salt, until they form stiff peaks. Whisk in 3 tablespoons sugar and bring back to stiff, glossy peaks.

6   Pile meringue on top of custard in rough peaks – do not attempt to spread meringue but make certain custard is completely covered.

7   Scatter remaining caster sugar and flaked almonds over meringue.

8   Bake in preheated oven for 25–30 minutes, until top of meringue is crisp with lightly golden peaks.

QUICK FOOLPROOF custard

SERVES 4

1 vanilla pod
600 ml (1 pint) double cream
5 egg yolks
1 level teaspoon cornflour
1 tablespoon caster sugar

The tiny amount of cornflour in the custard does not thicken it – it is merely a trick to prevent the eggs from curdling.

1   Split vanilla pod in half lengthwise. Scrape out seeds into double cream in a saucepan. Add pod as well.

2   Whisk egg yolks, cornflour and sugar together in a bowl.

3   Bring vanilla cream to boiling point. Remove pod. Allow cream to rise in pan, then pour quickly onto egg mixture, whisking continuously until mixture thickens.

4   Pass custard through a fine sieve – there you have it; quick, foolproof custard!

Should the custard look like curdling during reheating, quickly whisk in a tablespoon of double cream. This is a sure fire way of saving the custard – I know; I've done it many times!

peaches POACHED IN STRAWBERRY PUREE &

MUSCAT DE BEAUMES DE VENISE

SERVES 4

100 g (4 oz) strawberries
100 g (4 oz) caster sugar
300 ml (10 fl oz) water
half a bottle of Muscat de Beaume de Venise
1 vanilla pod
1 lemon
4 perfectly ripe peaches
iced water

A true summer pudding! It is essential to have perfectly ripe peaches for this dessert. Served with Cardamom & Honey Ice Cream (see recipe below) it oozes luscious, sensual flavours.

1 Hull strawberries. Purée fruit with sugar and water in a blender or food processor until smooth. Sieve into a pan.

2 Add wine and vanilla pod. Pare two strips lemon zest from lemon using a sharp knife. Add to pan. Bring to boil. Reduce to simmer.

3 Cut peaches in half and remove stones. Immerse fruit briefly (for no more than 30 seconds) in a bowl of boiling water. Remove fruit with a slotted spoon, plunge into iced water and slip off peach skins.

4 Add peaches to pan. Turn fruit over carefully in liquid, using two spoons. Poach gently for 3 minutes if peaches are perfectly ripe, or 5 minutes if they are slightly firm. Peaches should take on a pretty blush colour. Remove fruit from syrup when cooked.

5 Remove vanilla pod and lemon zest. Boil cooking syrup until reduced to a pale pink sauce. Taste and add a little more sugar if necessary. Cool and chill.

Serve the peaches with the chilled sauce, decorated with mint leaves which have been dusted with icing sugar. Cardamom & Honey Ice Cream is a perfect accompaniment.

cardamom & honey ICE CREAM

SERVES 4

10 egg yolks
100 g (4 oz) caster sugar
1 level teaspoon cornflour
100 g (4 oz) wild flower honey
850 ml (1½ pints) single cream
20 green cardamoms
600 ml (1 pint) double cream

Use the best honey you can buy – a local one if possible.

1 Blend egg yolks, sugar, cornflour, honey and a little single cream together in a large bowl.

2 Crush cardamoms, remove and grind seeds.

3 Bring single cream and cardamom seeds to boiling point. Gradually pour onto egg mixture, whisking constantly.

4 Rinse pan in cold water. Return custard to pan and cook very gently until it thickens and coats the back of a wooden spoon. Cool.

5 Lightly whisk double cream. Fold into cooled custard. Sieve into an ice cream churner or a shallow freezing box. Freeze following directions on page 154, for Caramel Ice Cream.

6 Use as required.

autumn

As summer fades we think
of the voluptuousness of
Autumn fruits and
vegetables. Early Autumn
suggests an abundance of
produce for the kitchen.
The golden russets and reds
of the orchard fruits, ripe
for picking and eating or for
turning into tarts, pies, ice-
creams and preserves.

As the smell of
woodsmoke pervades my
garden from the many
bonfires of prunings and
clippings, I think of smoked
meats, toffee apples and
collecting the new season's
walnuts. It is a busy time of
year and has a promise of its
own; a promise of a well-
stocked larder, richer more
mellow flavours, aromatic
herbs and the new season's
game.

spinach tagliatelle WITH MUSSELS

IN A GARLIC & THYME SAUCE

SERVES 4 AS A STARTER

Spinach Pasta made with 300 g (10 oz) flour (see page 147)

1.2 kg (2½ lb) fresh mussels in the shell
300 ml (10 fl oz) fish stock (see page 140)
2 cloves garlic
1 tablespoon chopped fresh chives
leaves from 6 sprigs fresh thyme
150 ml (5 fl oz) double cream
1 small red pepper
16 small florets broccoli
¼ teaspoon sugar
freshly ground black pepper

The essence of this dish is simplicity – we are capturing the clarity and freshness of the mussels. Try to buy Scottish rope-cultured mussels. They are cultivated in the pure water of the Scottish lochs, and are usually very plump for the size of the shell.

1   Make tagliatelle as described on page 147. Blanch in boiling salted water for 1 minute. Drain and rinse well under cold water to remove starchiness and keep strands separate.

2   Clean mussels, discard any broken or open ones and remove any beards – they just pull off.

3   Heat stock in a wide shallow pan. Tip in half cleaned mussels and cover pan. Cook quickly over high heat, shaking the pan, until mussels start to open. Remove immediately with draining spoon – work quickly; overcooking toughens mussels. Repeat with remaining mussels.

4   Remove mussels from shells with half a mussel shell or a teaspoon. Reserve juices and pour back into stock.

5   Crush garlic and add to pan with herbs and cream. Cook together to make sauce. Season carefully – remember the mussel juices will be quite salty!

6   Halve pepper and discard the core. Chop flesh – use only half if pepper is medium or large. Add to sauce with broccoli and cook for 2 or 3 minutes.

7   Add tagliatelle to pan, tossing in sauce, and heat through. Stir in reserved mussels and heat through. Check seasoning and serve.

This would make a lovely light lunch or supper dish if you increase the quantities by half.

carrot, honey AND ginger SOUP

This soup has a velvety texture – very comforting on cold days.

SERVES 4

450 g (1 lb) carrots
7.5 cm (3 inch) piece fresh root ginger
1 small onion
2 sticks celery
30 g (1 oz) unsalted butter
1 clove garlic
850 ml (1½ pints) water
2 teaspoons honey
1 bay leaf
salt and ground black pepper
150 ml (5 fl oz) double cream
Chopped fresh parsley or coriander to garnish

1 Peel and roughly chop all vegetables, including ginger. Melt butter in large pan, add vegetables and fry gently until soft. Add garlic.

2 Add water, honey and seasonings. Bring to boil. Simmer gently until vegetables are soft.

3 Remove bay leaf and liquidise soup. Rinse pan and return soup to it through medium sieve.

4 Reserve 2 tablespoons creams. Add remainder to soup and heat through. Check seasoning.

5 Serve in soup dishes. Add the reserved cream and swirl with the point of a knife. Scatter with a little chopped parsley or coriander.

crostini OF ROUILLE & GRUYERE

Serve these crostini with 'Old Vic' Fish Soup (page 74).

SERVES 4

CROSTINI:
1 baguette or loaf French bread
1 clove garlic
extra virgin olive oil

ROUILLE:
2 red peppers
2 tablespoons fresh breadcrumbs
4 tablespoons fish stock (page 140)
pinch saffron stamens
2 red chillies
2 small cloves garlic
½ teaspoon salt
freshly ground black pepper
1 teaspoon ground coriander seeds
1 tablespoon tomato purée
1 egg yolk
375 ml (12 fl oz) extra virgin olive oil
60 g (2 oz) grated Gruyère cheese

1 Preheat oven to 140C (275F/Gas 1).

2 Cut French bread into thin slices, then into finger shapes. Cut garlic and rub over bread, drizzle with olive oil. Place on a baking sheet and dry out in the oven for 10 minutes or so until crisp.

3 Raise oven temperature to 230C (450F/Gas 8). Roast and skin peppers in hot oven (see page 30). Cut in half, remove cores and seeds.

4 While peppers are roasting, soak breadcrumbs in fish stock and saffron. Remove cores and seeds from chillies. Peel garlic.

5 In a blender or food processor fitted with a metal blade purée roasted peppers and their juices, breadcrumbs, chillies, garlic, salt, pepper, coriander seeds, tomato puree and egg yolk. Add oil a little at a time through the feed tube with the motor running – as for mayonnaise – until rouille forms a thick emulsion.

6 Top the crostini (2 or 3 per person) with the rouille and sprinkle with a little grated Gruyère cheese.

7 Bake in a preheated oven at 220C (425F/Gas 7) for 2–3 minutes until cheese melts before serving.

'old vic' fish soup WITH PRAWNS, SCALLOPS, MUSSELS & FRESH HERBS

SERVES 4

150–180 g (5–6 oz) brill, turbot or cod
120 g (4 oz) salmon
salt and ground black pepper
16 mussels
4 uncooked Dublin Bay prawns
4 fresh scallops
150 ml (5 fl oz) white wine
600 ml (1 pint) reduced fish stock
(see page 140)
1 shallot
small bulb fennel
1 fat clove garlic
15 g (½ oz) unsalted butter
75 ml (2½ fl oz) double cream
1 tablespoon chopped fresh dill
1 tablespoon chopped fresh parsley and chives (mixed)
¼ teaspoon sugar

Once you have a well flavoured fish stock this soup is very quick and easy to make. The fish listed here are merely a suggestion – any fish can be used. Look for a blend of texture and colour, and try to include some good shellfish. Serve with Crostini of Rouille with Gruyere (page 73).

1   Wash, bone and skin fish. Cut each into four pieces. Season lightly.

2   Clean mussels and remove beards. Shell and de-vein prawns.

3   Clean scallops, discarding black sac and frill (your fishmonger will usually do this for you). Remove white sinew which holds scallop to shell. Wash coral. Slice scallops in half, into two discs.

4   Heat white wine in a wide based pan. Add mussels, cover pan and shake over the heat until shells open. Remove mussels with a slotted spoon. Leave 8 mussels on half shells. Remove rest from shells. Pass cooking liquor through a fine sieve to remove any grittiness and add to fish stock.

5   Finely dice shallot and fennel; peel and crush garlic. Cook vegetables in butter in a large pan until soft. Add fish stock and bring to boil.

6   Reduce heat to slow simmer. Add prawns and cook until they turn pink and are cooked through. Remove from pan. Add white fish and salmon – cook gently for 1 minute until slightly undercooked. Remove from pan. Drop in scallops and coral; cook for 30 seconds only. Remove from pan.

7   Reduce cooking liquor by boiling and add cream. Reduce until it has a deep flavour and velvety texture.

8   Throw in herbs, carefully stir in fish and shellfish and season adding sugar to taste, then serve immediately. Remember fish is slightly undercooked. Only a few seconds in hot soup will be necessary to finish cooking and heat it through.

pot roasted chicken WITH SAGE &

GLAZED ROOT VEGETABLES

**2 × 1.2 kg (2½ lb) corn-fed
chickens
5 or 6 sprigs sage
salt and ground black pepper
1 onion
1.7 litres (3 pints) white chicken
stock (page 141)
6 carrots
4 medium parsnips
3 or 4 sprigs summer savory
300 ml (10 fl oz) double cream
4 small leeks
chopped fresh parsley or chives,
to garnish**

A simple country dish with gutsy flavours.

1   Remove breasts from either side of chicken breast bones using a
   sharp, thin bladed filleting knife and by following the shape of the rib
   cage. Cut across breasts at wings to remove breasts from carcasses.

2   Cut legs and thighs from carcasses through ball and socket joints at
   thighs.

3   Make pockets in breasts behind fillets and insert a small sage leaf in
   each. Season chicken pieces.

4   Chop onion and heat with stock in a large pan until boiling. Add
   chicken legs, reduce heat and simmer gently for 15 minutes.

5   Peel and trim carrots and parsnips. Chop into thick slices.

6   Add half the sage and summer savory, prepared carrots and parsnips
   and chicken breasts to pan. Add a little more stock to cover if
   necessary. Cook for a further 15 minutes.

7   Remove chicken pieces and half the vegetables from pan with a slotted
   spoon. Purée the remainder in a liquidiser or food processor until
   smooth.

8   Rinse pan and return sauce to it through a sieve. Chop the remaining
   sage and summer savory. Stir in cream and chopped herbs. Season to
   taste. The texture should be silky and the flavour robust.

9   Trim leeks and cut into 5 cm (2 inch) pieces. Place the chicken with
   reserved vegetables and prepared leeks in a roasting tin and pour half
   sauce over and around.

10 Roast, uncovered, in preheated oven for 15 minutes or so, until
   chicken is cooked and vegetables have a nice golden glaze.

11 Heat remaining sauce. Serve chicken and vegetables with remaining
   sauce poured round. Garnish with a sprinkling of chopped parsley or
   chives.

*Save the carcasses to make white
chicken stock to freeze for next time.*

SESAME AND LIME SAUCE:
300 ml (10 fl oz) fish stock (see page 140)
1 piece star anise
2 limes
2 teaspoons honey
2 tablespoons corn oil
1 tablespoon sesame oil
salt and ground black pepper
handful chopped fresh coriander

SCALLOPS AND JOHN DORY:
12 large scallops
extra virgin olive oil, for searing
½ small red pepper
6 tablespoons fresh white breadcrumbs
1 tablespoon coriander seed
30 g (1 oz) butter
2 tablespoons extra virgin olive oil
4 × 150 g (5 oz) fillets John Dory (St Peter's fish)

CORIANDER CRUSTED john dory WITH scallops AND SESAME & LIME SAUCE

Fresh scallops are available from most good fishmongers, although you may have to order them two or three days in advance. If you are not sure how to shuck them, ask your supplier to do it for you (and you can watch for next time!). Never attempt to use frozen scallops – they look good until the ice has melted, when the texture totally breaks down.

1   Preheat oven to 220C (425F/Gas 7).

2   Prepare sauce. Place fish stock in a pan with star anise. Bring to boil then reduce by half.

3   Grate zest from limes and squeeze juice. Add both to stock with honey and boil again to reduce slightly. Mix the corn and sesame oils together and whisk into stock to form a thickened emulsion. Keep warm.

4   Check seasoning and add coriander leaves.

5   Prepare scallops. Remove corals and very white membrane which held scallops to shells.

6   Heat a skillet until very hot. Moisten some absorbent kitchen paper with olive oil and carefully rub over hot skillet.

7   Season scallops lightly. Sear both flat sides on hot skillet to give a golden crust. Set to one side.

8   Finely chop red pepper. Mix with breadcrumbs. Crush coriander seeds in a pestle and mortar or with end of a rolling pin. Sieve out shells and add ground seeds to pepper and breadcrumbs.

9   Heat butter and olive oil together in a small frypan, add breadcrumb mixture and fry until crumbs separate.

10 Season John Dory fillets and press crumbs onto top side. Place fillets in shallow roasting tin or baking sheet, crumb side up. Bake in preheated oven until topping is crispy and golden, about 5 minutes.

11 For last 1 minute place scallops on open tray with fillets to heat through. Do not overcook or they will toughen.

12 Gently reheat sauce. Serve John Dory and scallops with sauce poured round.

A simple stir-fry of vegetables, perhaps with a little ginger, would be perfect with this dish.

PAN FRIED calves' liver WITH PINK

PEPPERCORNS & BEETROOT DRESSING

Once the sauces are made the cooking of the calves' liver takes only moments in a very hot pan. This is stylish entertaining made easy!

1 Trim liver, removing and reserving any skin, veins and sinew.

2 Make dressing. Liquidise beetroot with stock. Heat gently with remaining ingredients in small pan. Whisk well and check seasoning. Serve hot but not boiling. The dressing will separate slightly to make a beautiful golden and red marbled effect on the plate.

3 Make sauce. Wash vegetables leaving skins on. Use half a small onion, half a stick celery and half a small carrot. Brown vegetables in skillet with butter.

4 Add liver trimmings and brown again.

5 Add half measured wine, boil and reduce down to sticky glaze.

6 Add remaining wine and sherry. Reduce again slightly. Add bay leaf and peppercorns. Simmer until sauce has good flavour. Strain into a clean pan.

7 Cut chilled butter into cubes and whisk into sauce to thicken and give a glossy appearance. Set to one side.

WHEN READY TO SERVE:

1 Reheat sauce and dressing.

2 Heat cast iron skillet until a very hot, even heat.

3 Swirl in butter and fry calves' liver briskly on both sides – about 30 seconds on each (less if very thinly sliced), for liver à point (pink in middle).

4 Serve on polenta (or mashed potato) with sauce poured over and dressing poured round (see photograph above).

SERVES 4 AS A STARTER

250 g (9 oz) calves' liver, thinly sliced
30 g (1 oz) unsalted butter

DRESSING:
1 small cooked beetroot
2 tablespoons white chicken stock (see page 141)
leaves from two sprigs fresh thyme
60 ml (2 fl oz) extra virgin olive oil
1 tablespoon balsamic vinegar
1 teaspoon pink peppercorns
salt and ground black pepper

SAUCE:
1 small onion
1 small stick celery
1 small carrot
30 g (1 oz) unsalted butter
150 ml (5 fl oz) red wine
1 tablespoon amontillado sherry
1 bay leaf
5 or 6 black peppercorns
15 g (½ oz) chilled unsalted butter
mashed potato or creamed polenta to serve (page 146)

Pan Fried Calves' Liver

fillet of fallow deer FLAVOURED

WITH JUNIPER & PORT

SERVES 4

**1 fillet off the saddle, weighing
550–675g (1¼–1½ lb)
2 or 3 sprigs thyme or summer
savory
extra virgin olive oil
1 glass red wine
½ glass port
2 bay leaves
juniper berries
300 ml (10 fl oz) reduced stock
unsalted butter, chilled
salt and ground black pepper**

*Serve with Pasta Noodles (page 147),
Mulled Pears (page 148) and Parsnip
Chips.*

Fallow deer is not easy to come by, but is worth seeking out for a special occasion. Make sure it has been well hung before you buy it, in which case it will be meltingly tender with a well developed, rounded flavour. Ask your butcher or game dealer to take a fillet off one side of the saddle of a small fallow or roe deer.

1   Preheat oven to 240C (475F/Gas 9).

2   Trim off the loose chain of meat, all cartilage and skin tissue. Use to make stock (see page 140) and reduce to give a good flavour.

3   Make a few incisions down the length of fillet, insert tiny sprigs thyme or summer savory. Rub all over with olive oil.

4   Heat a cast iron pan or griddle until evenly hot. Sear fillet on all sides until a good brown colour. Transfer fillet to roasting tin. Flash roast for 10 minutes in preheated oven – this will leave venison nicely pink in the middle. Remove and keep hot in a warming oven to rest meat.

5   Add wine and port to pan and boil until reduced and the pan is deglazed. Add bay leaves, juniper and approximately 300 ml (10 fl oz) reduced stock, scraping all meat juices into stock. Reduce to give good flavour. Strain into clean pan.

6   Add knobs of chilled butter until sauce is thick enough, has a deep colour and good gloss. Correct seasoning.

7   Slice fillet on a slight diagonal – this presents meat at its most tender – overlap slices on a serving plate. Spoon sauce over.

parsnip chips

SERVES 4

**2 parsnips
sunflower oil, for deep-fat frying
salt**

1   Peel parsnips. Slice very thinly down length of root – a mandolin is best for this. Rub dry in a cloth.

2   Heat sunflower oil in a deep pan to 180C (350F) and test for frying temperature with a bread cube – it should brown quickly and float on top whilst cooking. Deep fry parsnip until golden. This will only take seconds. Drain on absorbent kitchen paper. Sprinkle lightly with salt and keep warm until ready to serve.

AUBERGINE & PUMPKIN satay

SERVES 4

KEBABS:
4 thick slices aubergine
4 thick slices pumpkin
1 yellow pepper
sesame oil
salt and ground black pepper
coriander seeds

SATAY SAUCE:
1 red chilli
1 tablespoon ground almonds
1 tablespoon peanut kernels
(skinned)
dash soy sauce
1 teaspoon tomato purée
dash Worcestershire sauce
1 teaspoon redcurrant jelly
2 or 3 drops Tabasco
1 tablespoon single cream

This is an interesting vegetarian dish with Pacific Rim flavours. Serve with Fragrant Rice (page 145), Hot Sesame Potato Cakes (page 145) and Sweet Chilli Sauce.

1 Preheat oven to 220C (425F/Gas 7).

2 Prepare kebabs. Cut aubergine and pumpkin into cubes about 3 cm (just over 1 inch) in size. Leave black skin on aubergine.

3 Cut pepper in half, remove core, seeds and membrane. Cut flesh into pieces of same size as aubergine. Thread vegetables alternately onto wooden skewers. Allow two skewers per person.

4 Rub vegetables with sesame oil. Season with salt and pepper. Crush coriander seeds and sprinkle over vegetables.

5 Roast on a baking sheet in preheated oven for 12–15 minutes, until cooked through and starting to blacken at edges. Turn skewers over once during cooking to keep vegetables moist and ensure even cooking. Baste with the sesame oil.

6 Prepare satay sauce. Cut chilli in half and remove core. Use one quarter of flesh only – chop finely. Purée all sauce ingredients in a blender or food processor with 3 tablespoons cold water. Check seasoning. Cook gently in a small saucepan for 4 or 5 minutes.

7 Serve Aubergine & Pumpkin Satay with sauce spooned over.

sweet chilli SAUCE

SERVES 4

1 small onion
1 fat clove garlic
1 stick celery
1 small eating apple
1 small red pepper
1 red chilli
8 tomatoes
extra virgin olive oil
2 teaspoons tomato purée
dash soy sauce
dash Worcestershire Sauce
1 tablespoon demerara sugar
salt and ground black pepper

1 Peel and finely chop half onion. Crush garlic. Finely chop celery. Peel, core and chop apple. Cut pepper in half, remove core and chop flesh. Cut chilli, remove core and finely chop half the flesh. Skin tomatoes (see page 48). Cut into halves, scoop out seeds and chop flesh.

2 Heat some oil in a frying pan, add prepared vegetables and fry until soft. Add remaining ingredients with 150ml (5 fl oz) cold water and simmer together to form a chunky, well-flavoured sauce.

Serve these with Hot Sesame Potato Cakes (page 145).

CARAMELISED & ROASTED tomato tarts

SERVES 4

180 g (6 oz) Old Vic Foolproof Pastry (see page 152)

8 sun dried tomatoes in oil
4 large sprigs fresh basil
4 tablespoons sweet pepper marmalade (see recipe below)
8 ripe plum tomatoes
salt and ground black pepper
extra virgin olive oil
4 stoned black olives
mixed salad leaves, to serve

I like to serve Rocket Purée (see page 151) and Avocado Salsa (page 149) with the Caramelised Tomato Tarts.

In Britain we can only make really flavourful tomato dishes in early autumn, when our tomatoes have ripened naturally on the plants rather than in transit. The flavour of these tarts is so pure – it is one of my favourite recipes – I hope you like it.

1 Preheat oven to 190C (375F/Gas 5).

2 Roll out pastry to line four individual 10 cm (4 inch) tart tins. Prick the bases with a fork and bake blind for 15 minutes in preheated oven (see page 105).

3 Increase oven temperature to 220C (425F/Gas 7).

4 Skin sun dried tomatoes. Cover with boiling water and leave for 10 minutes. Drain, rinse under cold water and peel away skins. Chop basil. Mix both with sweet pepper marmalade in a small bowl.

5 Divide pepper mixture between prepared tart tins. Slice tomatoes and season. Arrange attractively over pepper filling, then drizzle with olive oil. Halve olives and arrange on top.

6 Bake in preheated oven for 5 minutes until tomato is just starting to blacken and appear roasted. (This can be enhanced by a quick blast under a hot grill, or with a blow torch.)

7 Serve the tarts with a garnish of mixed salad leaves.

sweet pepper MARMALADE

2 red peppers
2 yellow peppers
2 orange peppers
1 onion
1 fat clove garlic
3 tablespoons extra virgin olive oil
8 green cardamoms
2 tablespoons white wine vinegar
2 tablespoons brown sugar
½ teaspoon Tabasco or hot chilli sauce
salt and ground black pepper

This is a sweet, sour and mildly spiced relish with many different uses.

1 Roast and skin peppers (see page 30). Cut flesh into long, thin strips.

2 Peel onion and slice finely. Peel and crush garlic. Fry together in olive oil in a large frying pan until soft.

3 Crush cardamoms and remove seeds. Crush seeds and add them to onions with peppers, wine vinegar, sugar and Tabasco.

4 Simmer gently for about 25–30 minutes, until all ingredients have softened and caramelised, and flavours have mellowed.

5 Season with salt and lots of freshly ground black pepper.

*Caramelised & roasted tomato tarts
Avocado salsa page 149.*

82

HOT SMOKED sea bass OVER ROSEMARY

A lovely dish with smoky aromas – just right for Autumn days.

SERVES 4 AS A STARTER

1 sea bass, about 600g (1¼ lb)
salt and ground black pepper
extra virgin olive oil
30 g (1 oz) unsalted butter
6 sprigs fresh rosemary

In the restaurant I serve this with Saffron Risotto Cakes (see below) and Oregano Sauce (page 151).

1 Preheat oven to 220C (425F/Gas 7).

2 Ask your fishmonger to scale and fillet the bass, leaving the pretty blue skin on. Cut each fillet in half. Season the flesh of the fish and rub olive oil into the skin.

3 Set up a smoker (see page 25) and strew the base with 5 sprigs of rosemary. Cover with the lid and heat until a steady stream of aromatic smoke is produced. Place the bass fillets skin side down on the grid and replace the lid. Smoke for 3 minutes to allow flavour to permeate fish without cooking it through. Remove from smoker.

4 Place butter on a flat roasting tray. Sit fillets on top, skin uppermost. Cook the bass in preheated oven for 3 to 4 minutes, until just cooked through and moist. Serve garnished with remaining rosemary.

saffron RISOTTO CAKES

These may be prepared in advance and reheated on a baking sheet at 220C (425F/Gas 7) for 3 or 4 minutes.

SERVES 4

3 tablespoons extra virgin olive oil
1 tablespoon finely chopped onion
125 g (4 oz) Arborio rice
1 small red pepper
1 small courgette
1 clove garlic
1 pinch saffron stamens
600 ml (1 pint) fish stock
salt and ground black pepper

1 Heat 1 tablespoon oil in a pan, add onion and fry until soft. Add rice and stir.

2 Cut pepper in half, discard core and chop finely – only use half the pepper if it is medium or large. Finely dice courgette and peel and crush garlic. Add vegetables to pan.

3 Infuse saffron in stock and stir gradually into pan. Bring to boil. Reduce to barely simmering and heat until rice is cooked, shaking the pan frequently, giving a moist, glutinous risotto. Season to taste.

4 Spread thickly (3.5 cm/1½ inches deep) in a dish, leave to go quite cold and set. Either cut into 4 squares or 4 circles using a 5 cm (2 inch) plain cutter.

5 Fry the risotto cakes in a frypan in remaining 2 tablespoons olive oil, until both sides are crisp and golden.

tomato & olive DRESSING

4 fresh bay leaves
a handful fresh chives
3 cloves garlic
10 tomatoes
1 red pepper
3 parsley stalks
4 large sprigs fresh basil
2 strips lemon zest
600 ml (1 pint) extra virgin olive oil
60 ml (2 fl oz) white wine vinegar
2 teaspoons salt
freshly ground black pepper
4 teaspoons sugar

This needs to be started the day before it is required. It will keep well in the refrigerator for use another time. It also freezes well.

1 Tear bay leaves in half and tear chives. Peel and roughly chop garlic. Scrape seeds from tomatoes and roughly chop flesh. Cut pepper in half and remove core. Roughly chop flesh. Place bay leaves, chives, garlic, tomatoes, pepper, parsley, basil, lemon zest, oil, vinegar, salt, pepper and sugar in a large bowl. Cover and leave in refrigerator overnight for flavours to infuse.

2 Press through a coarse sieve into a clean saucepan to form a dressing. Heat gently and check seasoning. Whisk well to emulsify before serving.

roast fillet of cod STUDDED WITH

GARLIC & PROSCIUTTO

SERVES 4

4 × 250 g (9 oz) pieces cod fillet
1 fat clove garlic
4 thick slices prosciutto
8 leaves fresh basil
salt and ground black pepper
3 tablespoons extra virgin olive oil
4 thin courgettes

I like to serve this dish with Tomato & Olive Dressing (see recipe above). Serve with Saffron Noodles (page 147) and some Tapenade (page 150). Most fishmongers will skin the cod for you if you ask.

1 Preheat oven to 220C (425F/Gas 7).

2 Skin the cod fillets. Remove any bones with tweezers. Peel garlic and cut into slivers and cut prosciutto into batons. Tear basil leaves into pieces.

3 Make horizontal slits in cod with a small knife. Place a piece of garlic, prosciutto and basil in each slit. Repeat until each piece of cod has five or six insertions of ham and herbs. Season cod fillets with salt and pepper. Smooth a little olive oil into each fillet.

4 Heat a cast iron skillet until hot. Press fillets, flesh side downwards, onto hot skillet to form a golden crust. Transfer cod to a roasting tin.

5 Roast in preheated oven for 4–5 minutes, depending on thickness of fish.

6 While cod is roasting, trim and slice courgettes and sauté in remaining olive oil in a skillet. Season and transfer to centre of warmed serving plates.

7 Rest roasted cod on courgettes. Serve with Tomato & Olive Dressing.

pot roasted duck WITH FRESH FIGS

2 lean ducks
3 or 4 sprigs sage
1 onion
2 carrots
1 leek
2 sticks celery
5 tablespoons amontillado sherry
150 ml (5 fl oz) red wine
850 ml (30 fl oz) duck stock
1 bay leaf
4 fresh figs
90 g (3 oz) chilled unsalted butter

Most good greengrocers and supermarkets sell fresh figs in the autumn. You may use either the green or dark purple varieties to equal effect. I buy Gressingham or Barbary ducks.

1   Preheat the oven to 180C (350F/Gas 4).

2   Remove the breasts and legs from ducks, removing and reserving skin from breasts. Make a stock from carcasses and simmer slowly (see page 141).

3   Stuff duck breast with sage, tucking it in behind fillets.

4   Peel and roughly chop vegetables.

5   Heat a frypan or skillet and fry skins from breasts to release fat. Remove skins. Add prepared vegetables to pan and brown in duck fat. Add sherry and reduce to a sticky consistency. Add wine and reduce again.

6   Add stock to pan with bay leaf and bring to boil. Pour into ovenproof dish.

7   Peel and roughly chop two figs. Add to dish then lay duck legs on top, skin side up. Pot roast, uncovered, in preheated oven for 40 minutes.

8   Lay duck breasts on top of vegetables and baste with juices. Cook for further 10 minutes. Legs should be well done and crispy and breasts just nicely pink. Remove duck and keep hot.

9   Strain stock from dish through sieve, pressing vegetables and figs through to extract all possible flavour. Return to pan and reduce over high heat to give good flavour.

10 Reduce heat and whisk in sufficient butter to thicken sauce and give a glossy appearance. Season to taste.

11 Cut remaining figs into quarters. Heat figs through in sauce. Serve around duck on serving plate.

This recipe is excellent served with griddled Corn Cakes (page 146) and perhaps some stir-fried green vegetable.

escabêche of partridge WITH

WALNUTS & OLOROSSO SHERRY

2 oven ready partridge
1 bay leaf
4 sprigs fresh thyme
150 ml (5 fl oz) brown chicken
stock (see page 140)

SAUCE:
30 g (1 oz) unsalted butter
partridge carcasses and legs
1 tablespoon dry Olorosso sherry
150 ml (5 fl oz) red wine
a few black peppercorns
4 or 5 crushed juniper berries
¼ teaspoon arrowroot
salt

MARINADE:
1 stick celery
4 spring onions
1 small carrot
1 small courgette
1 small red pepper
1 small yellow pepper
300 ml (10 fl oz) walnut oil
2 tablespoons balsamic vinegar
150 ml (5 fl oz) sauce – see above
1 tablespoon walnut halves,
blanched and skinned
salt and ground black pepper

This is derived from a dish I ate in Andalucia and which I find translates very well for use with English grey-leg partridge; small birds with plump little breasts and lots of flavour. You poach the birds in stock and herbs then marinate them overnight. The result is moist and full of flavour. This is a great dinner party starter or middle course since it is all done the day before. On the night, all you do is put it on a plate!

1   Cut down either side of breast bones of partridges and carefully remove breasts.

2   Make a lengthwise incision under fillets of breasts to make a pocket. Tuck inside a piece of fresh bay leaf and a sprig of thyme. Remove skin from breasts.

3   Heat chicken stock in a frypan, add partridge breasts and poach gently for 2 or 3 minutes each side, until cooked but still quite pink in the middle. Remove partridge from stock.

4   Prepare sauce. Melt butter in a large pan and brown carcasses and legs. Add sherry and reduce over high heat until liquid is sticky. Gradually add wine, reducing between each addition. Add chicken stock peppercorns and juniper berries, reduce until a good flavour.

5   Blend arrowroot with a little water, whisk into sauce, boil and check for flavour. Reserve sauce to add to marinade.

6   Prepare marinade. Finely chop celery and spring onions. Peel carrot and dice with courgette. Cut peppers in half and discard cores. Chop flesh – use only half of each pepper if medium or large. Fry vegetables in a pan with a little walnut oil – keep them crisp and colours bright.

7   Add vinegar and bring to boil. Add measured sauce, remaining walnut oil, walnuts and seasoning and whisk until blended.

8   Pour into a deep container and submerge partridge breasts in marinade. Cool then cover and place in refrigerator for at least 12 hours.
    The next day, serve partridge thinly sliced with a little of the vegetables and marinade as accompaniments.

braised oxtail

2 oxtails, cut into pieces
2 tablespoons seasoned flour
beef dripping or butter
1 onion
2 sticks celery
2 medium carrots
1 leek
150 ml (5 fl oz) ruby port
1 bottle red wine (a full bodied
Rhône would be good)
1.2 litre (2 pints) rich beef stock
(see page 141)
2 sticks cinnamon, broken into
pieces
3 bay leaves
1 teaspoon black peppercorns
5 or 6 sprigs thyme
4 or 5 crushed juniper berries
3 cloves
salt and ground black pepper

If possible cook the oxtail the day before it is required. It can then be well chilled and the resultant layer of fat lifted from the surface before reheating and finishing the sauce. Ask your butcher to chop the oxtails into pieces for you.

1 Preheat oven to 150C (300F/Gas 2).

2 Trim oxtail pieces of any excess fat and wash the meat. Toss in seasoned flour and shake off any excess.

3 Melt some dripping or butter in a heavy-bottomed pan or frying pan. Add oxtail; sear and brown on all sides. Remove oxtail with slotted spoon to deep ovenproof casserole.

4 Peel and roughly chop vegetables, add to pan and brown in dripping or butter. Add vegetables to oxtail in casserole.

5 Add port to pan. Reduce until sticky, stirring constantly to scrape up crusty meat sediment from pan.

6 Gradually add wine to pan and bring to boil. Boil hard for about 10 minutes to drive off alcohol. Add stock, cinnamon, bay, peppercorns, thyme, juniper, cloves, salt and pepper. Return to boil. Add to oxtail casserole.

7 Cover with lid and cook in preheated oven for 3½–4 hours, until meat is falling from bones.

8 Remove oxtail from casserole with slotted spoon and keep hot. Strain casserole juices into clean pan, pressing vegetables well with back of ladle or draining spoon to extract all possible flavour. At this point the casserole could be refrigerated overnight to allow the fat to solidify, and then be removed. Reheat oxtail and sauce.

9 Bring sauce to boil and season to taste. Skim off as much fat as possible. Sauce should be deep in colour, rich and unctuous.

10 Serve oxtail with sauce poured over and Mashed Potatoes with Olive Oil (page 144).

Some stir-fried root vegetables tossed in parsley make an excellent accompaniment.

LEFT
Fillet of lamb on couscous with skewers of
roast vegetables and lambs' kidneys

ABOVE
Braised oxtail and mashed potatoes with
olive oil

fillet of lamb ON COUSCOUS

SERVES 4

GARNISH FOR COUSCOUS:
1 small onion
1 clove garlic
2 tablespoons extra virgin olive oil
60 g (2 oz) blanched almonds
12 no-soak dried apricots
½ teaspoon coriander seed
2 tablespoons chopped fresh chives
1 tablespoon chopped fresh coriander

FILLET OF LAMB:
2 fillets from a small saddle of lamb
2 sprigs rosemary
1 clove garlic
extra virgin olive oil
salt and ground black pepper

COUSCOUS:
125 g (4 oz) couscous
150 ml (5 fl oz) vegetable or white chicken stock (page 141)
pinch saffron stamens

SAUCE:
1 glass red wine
300 ml (10 fl oz) reduced lamb stock (see page 141)
30 g (1 oz) chilled unsalted butter
2 tablespoons double cream
1 tablespoon wholegrain mustard

This may be served with Skewers of Roast Vegetable and Lamb's Kidney (page 93). Prepare them in advance and cook them in the hot oven, once the lamb has been set to rest in the warming oven.

This lamb dish has a Middle Eastern flavour which is just right for summer. We serve it on a bed of couscous, which requires only brief cooking – it is very light to eat.

Get your butcher to cut you two fillets from either side of a small saddle of young lamb.

1   Preheat oven to 220C (425F/Gas 7).

2   Prepare garnishes for couscous. Peel half a small onion and chop finely. Peel and crush garlic. Heat olive oil in a small pan and cook onion and garlic until soft but not browned. Toast almonds under a hot grill until browned. Chop apricots and add to onions with almonds. Crush coriander seed and add to chopped herbs. Keep until required.

3   Prepare lamb. Make tiny incisions with tip of a knife along lamb fillet. Break 1 stem rosemary into small sprigs. Peel garlic and cut into slivers. Insert rosemary and garlic into lamb. Rub fillets with olive oil and season with salt and pepper. Heat a skillet or cast iron frying pan. Sear lamb on all sides.

4   Transfer lamb to a roasting tin and cook for 6–7 minutes only. Put to rest on a plate in a warming oven for a further 10-12 minutes. This will give very pink, but not rare, lamb. As season progresses and lamb gets older, cooking time will need to be increased.

5   As soon as lamb goes into oven start couscous. Place grains in a large bowl. Bring vegetable or white chicken stock to boil in a pan with saffron. Pour boiling stock over couscous, stir with a fork to separate grains and season lightly. Leave to stand, covered, for 10-15 minutes, until grains are swollen and fluffy.

6   Prepare sauce. Pour wine into the roasting tin and place over a medium heat. Bring to boil, scraping any meat sediment up into sauce. Boil until reduced and sticky. Add lamb stock and remaining rosemary. Reduce again by half. Whisk in chilled butter, a little at a time, to give a glossy sauce. Season to taste with salt and pepper.

7   Pour half lamb sauce into a separate pan. Whisk in cream and mustard. Cook for 2 or 3 minutes, until slightly reduced, to allow flavours to blend.

8   Add garnishes, coriander and herbs to couscous. Slice lamb fillets diagonally.

9   Divide couscous between four plates. Arrange overlapping slices of lamb around couscous. Pour lamb sauce around meat and mustard sauce around couscous, or over skewers of Roast Vegetables and Lambs' Kidneys (see page 93).

SKEWERS OF roast vegetables AND

LAMBS' KIDNEYS

These may be served as a simple supper dish on a bed of couscous, or as a vegetable garnish to Fillet of Lamb on Couscous (page 92).

1 lemon
1 green chilli
2 tablespoons extra virgin olive oil
1 tablespoon mustard seed
2 teaspoons coriander seed
salt and ground black pepper
1 red pepper
1 yellow pepper
1 small aubergine
1 courgette
4 lambs' kidneys

1   Preheat oven to 220C (425F/Gas 7).

2   Squeeze juice from half lemon into a bowl. Cut chilli in half, remove core and seeds and finely chop flesh. Add chilli, oil and mustard seed to lemon juice. Crush coriander seed and add with seasonings.

3   Cut peppers in half and remove core, seeds and membrane. Cut into 2.5 cm (1 inch) squares.

4   Trim aubergine and slice thickly. Cut slices into quarters, leaving skin on. Layer in a colander with salt and leave for 10 minutes to extract bitter juices. Rinse thoroughly under cold running water. Pat dry.

5   Cut courgette into thick slices. Skin kidneys, if necessary. Snip away hard white core using scissor tips. Cut kidneys in half.

6   Thread vegetables and kidneys onto 4 wooden satay sticks. Marinate in the spiced oil for 30 minutes, turning and basting from time to time.

7   Rest sticks across a small baking dish, suspending vegetables over dish. Brush with marinade and season with salt and pepper.

8   Roast in preheated oven for 10–15 minutes until vegetables and kidneys are cooked and have an attractive charred appearance. Baste and turn once during cooking.

The vegetable sticks could also be cooked under a very hot grill.

SAGE SMOKED pork fillet WITH BROCCOLI & PANCETTA

SERVES 4

2 fillets of pork
6 or 7 stems sage leaves
salt and ground black pepper
2 heads broccoli
12 pitted prunes
extra virgin olive oil

BROCCOLI & PANCETTA:
12 strips pancetta
2 tablespoons pine kernels
chilled unsalted butter

This has welcoming flavours reminiscent of Tuscany when served with Creamed Polenta (page 146) and Pickled Plums (page 148).

1   Preheat oven to 240C (475F/Gas 9).

2   Trim pork fillet of all sinew, fat and scrappy ends – use to make stock which you need for the sauce (see page 141).

3   Set up smoker (page 25). Add the stems of sage, cover and heat until steady stream of smoke is given off. Season pork and sit fillets on wire rack. Place in smoker; replace lid. Smoke one side for 3 minutes, turn, smoke second side for 3 minutes. Remove from smoker.

4   Break broccoli into florets and chop prunes while pork is smoking.

5   Smear pork fillets with olive oil, sit on remaining sage in roasting tin. Roast in preheated oven for 5 minutes. Allow to rest for 5 minutes.

6   Cook the pancetta in a dry frying pan over a high heat until very crisp. No fat is required. Set to one side.

7   Heat some olive oil in frying pan. Add pine kernels, cook until golden. Add prunes, allow to plump up in oil. Remove with slotted spoon. Add broccoli to pan, stir-fry until cooked. Return pine kernels and prunes to pan, season lightly.

8   Strain pork stock, return to pan and boil rapidly until reduced. Whisk chilled butter into stock to thicken. Season.

Sweet Pepper Marmalade (page 82) also goes well with this dish.

9   Slice pork fillet diagonally, serve with slices overlapped. Pour a little sauce over and serve with broccoli with crisp pancetta on top.

roast duckling WITH BLACK BEAN

SERVES 4

2 × 1.6 kg (3 lb 4 oz) oven ready
Barbary Ducklings
4 sage leaves
salt and ground black pepper
1 tablespoon red plum jam
1 tablespoon honey
1 tablespoon dark soy sauce

SAUCE:
250 g (9 oz) black beans
4 spring onions
1 red chilli
1 clove garlic
1 tablespoon extra olive oil
2 tablespoons reduced duck stock
(page 141)
1 tablespoon dark soy sauce
1 tablespoon brown sugar
1 tablespoon sesame oil

Although I always like to use British products our Aylesbury duck has too much flabby fat for this dish. Gressingham duck will not do either because the legs are more like Mallard and the skin hasn't enough fat to go very crispy. We use free-range Barbary duck. It has more meat to carcass than the ducks we are used to, and the fat cooks beautifully crisp.

1 Start this recipe the day before you intend to eat it. Pour boiling water over ducks in clean bowl or sink to scald them. Tie legs together with a looped piece of string and hang ducks in a cool, airy place overnight. This helps skin to give off its fat and become very crisp. Soak black beans for the sauce overnight.

2 Preheat oven to 220C (425F/Gas 7). Rinse beans and cook them in boiling water as directed on packet.

3 Using a sharp filleting knife, cut down either side of duck breastbones and, allowing knife to slide along rib cage, remove breasts. Make one slit under each breast fillet and insert a small sage leaf. Season breasts and set to one side.

4 Take off legs at thigh joint. Season. Heat jam, honey, 1 tablespoon soy sauce and 3 tablespoon water together until melted. Boil until reduced to make a glaze. Paint legs with some of glaze. Use remaining carcasses to make a well-flavoured stock (page 140).

5 Roast legs in a tin in preheated oven for 40–45 minutes, until skin is crisp and easily lifts off. Flesh should be well done.

6 Complete sauce while duck is roasting. Drain black beans. Trim and finely chop spring onions. Cut chilli in half, remove core and seeds and finely chop flesh. Crush garlic. Fry vegetables and black beans in olive oil in a frying pan until vegetables are soft. Add duck stock, remaining soy sauce and sugar then stir in sesame oil. Season to taste.

7 Prepare breasts about 15 minutes before duck legs should be cooked. Score fat finely all over with a sharp knife. Paint breasts with remaining glaze.

8 Heat a skillet or cast iron frying pan to a very hot, even heat. Sear duck breasts, skin side down, until fat flows and skin crisps. Remove breasts to roasting tin with legs and roast for 7–10 minutes, dependent on thickness. Rest in a warming oven for 10 minutes. Reheat black bean sauce.

9 Slice duck breasts diagonally and serve on a bed of black bean sauce.

Serve crispy duck legs with breasts, or shred meat from bone and crispy skin and use both to fill Peking Pancakes (page 97), to serve with the duckling and black bean sauce.

peking pancakes & HOI SIN SAUCE

PANCAKES:
250 g (8 oz) plain flour
250 ml (8 fl oz) boiling water
2 tablespoons sesame oil

7.5 cm (3 inch) piece cucumber
8 spring onions
flour, for dusting

HOI SIN SAUCE:
1 clove garlic
6 spring onions
2 red chillies
1 piece stem ginger
1 tablespoon soy sauce
2 tablespoons plum jam
1 teaspoon tomato purée
salt and ground black pepper
2 tablespoons sesame oil

These make an excellent accompaniment to Roast Duckling with Black Bean Sauce (page 96). Fill with roast, shredded duck meat — that from the legs of the previous recipe is ideal.

1 Prepare pancakes. Sieve flour into a mixing bowl and add boiling water and 1 teaspoon sesame oil. Mix to a dough then turn onto a lightly floured surface and knead until smooth. Cover with plastic wrap or foil and leave to rest for 30 minutes.

2 Divide dough into walnut sized pieces and flatten each piece with heel of your hand to a 7.5 cm (3 inch) disc. Brush each disc with sesame oil.

3 Place one disc on top of another, two oiled sides together. Dust lightly with flour. Roll out pair of pancakes to about 13 cm (5 inches). You will need at least two pancakes per person.

4 Heat a non-stick frying pan, cast iron pan or griddle to an even heat. Cook a pair of pancakes in pan for 60–90 seconds, until bubbly and slightly golden. Flip pancakes over and cook second side for 60–90 seconds.

5 Gently tear pancakes apart. Cover and keep warm so that they remain pliable while cooking remaining pancakes.

6 Shred cucumber and 8 spring onions. Set to one side.

7 Make sauce while pancakes are cooking. Crush garlic. Trim and finely slice spring onions. Cut chillies in half, remove core and seeds and finely chop flesh. Dice ginger. Place garlic, spring onions, chillies, ginger, soy sauce, jam, tomato puree, salt, pepper and sesame oil in a small pan with 2 teaspoons water and simmer together to make a hot, sweet sauce.

8 Serve pancakes with duck meat, crispy skin, shredded cucumber and spring onion. Place a little of each in a pancake and top with sauce. Roll up, ready to eat.

The pancakes may be filled by you in the kitchen, or by your guests at the table.

mascarpone cheesecake

SERVES 4

BASE:
280 g (10 oz) plain chocolate
digestive biscuits
75 g (2½ oz) walnuts
100 g (3½ oz) unsalted butter

CHEESECAKE:
420 g (15 oz) mascarpone
½ teaspoon natural vanilla essence
2 lemons
3 eggs, size 2
200 g (7 oz) caster sugar
150 ml (5 fl oz) fresh soured
cream
freshly grated nutmeg
dark chocolate curls, to decorate

*This unusual, elegant cheesecake needs no fruit topping for
embellishment. A few bitter chocolate curls are all that is required.*

1   Preheat oven to 150C (300F/Gas 2).

2   Prepare base. Crush digestive biscuits in a plastic bag or between sheets
    of baking parchment with a rolling pin. Finely chop walnuts. Melt
    butter in a saucepan, add biscuits and walnuts and mix well. Press into
    base of a greased 25 cm (10 inch) flan tin. Chill well.

3   Prepare cheesecake. Whisk together mascarpone and vanilla essence
    with grated zest from two lemons and juice from one and a half, to
    form a soft, smooth, floppy mixture.

4   Whisk eggs and sugar together with a mixer until they form a thick
    trail which will stay on the surface. Gently mix egg mixture into cheese
    mixture, using a balloon whisk or spatula. Pour onto the biscuit base,
    filling tin right to the top.

5   Bake in preheated oven for 30 minutes. Cool in oven with door ajar.
    While still warm pour soured cream over surface. Dust with nutmeg.
    Chill. Decorate with chocolate curls.

*Plum and honey mousse with walnut
shortbread (recipes on page 100)*

plum and honey mousse

WITH CINNAMON

SERVES 4

450 g (1 lb) plums
1 lemon
cinnamon stick
3 or 4 tablespoons wild flower
honey, according to the sweetness
of plums
4 leaves gelatine
150 ml (5 fl oz) double cream
2 large egg whites
chopped shelled pistachios

Use dessert plums for this dish – our own yellow fleshed Victorias give a good flavour although some of the redder dessert varieties such as Czar give a pretty pink colour. Serve with Walnut Shortbread.

1   Halve and stone plums. Cook in a saucepan with juice from lemon, 3 tablespoons water and a small piece of cinnamon stick for 20 minutes, or until very soft. Remove cinnamon.

2   Purée in a blender or food processor and sieve into a clean pan. Add honey and stir until dissolved.

3   Soften gelatine leaves in cold water, squeeze dry. Add to fruit purée and stir until dissolved. Pour into a bowl and chill in freezer until on point of setting.

4   Whisk cream in a bowl to a soft, floppy consistency and fold into purée.

5   Whisk egg whites in a clean bowl until stiff. Fold into mixture to form a light mousse. Pour into pretty glasses and top with chopped pistachios.

walnut shortbread

SERVES 4

120 g (4 oz) softened unsalted
butter
60 g (2 oz) caster sugar
30 g (1 oz) walnuts
120 g (4 oz) plain flour
60 g (2 oz) semolina
caster sugar, to dredge

Walnut Shortbreads make a lovely accompaniment to mousses, fruit salads and ice cream. It is a very fragile dough which is why it is so crumbly and rich to eat. The dough must be handled lightly and carefully. Heavy handling will cause the butter to oil out and the biscuits will then be hard instead of crisp and crumbly.

Shortbread couldn't be quicker or simpler to make, provided you start with softened butter.

1   Preheat oven to 150C (300F/Gas 2). Grease a baking sheet.

2   Cream butter and sugar together in a mixing bowl until light in colour and fluffy in texture.

3   Finely chop walnuts, mix with flour and semolina. Gradually work dry mixture into creamed butter until it forms a dough. Blend in final few crumbs with your hand to make it all stick together. Gently knead until smooth.

4   Roll out lightly on a floured surface to a rectangle about 5 mm (¼ inch) thick. Cut shortbread into fingers and place on prepared baking sheet.

5   Crimp edges with back of a fork and prick shortbread with a fork in neat lines. This is partly tradition and partly to prevent the biscuits from bubbling up. Cut into finger shapes.

6   Bake in preheated oven for 10–12 minutes until a pale golden colour. Dredge with caster sugar and leave on baking sheet to cool. The biscuits only become crisp when cold.

passion fruit soufflé

If you have a surfeit of egg whites, do freeze them for later use. They will whisk up to an amazing volume if you use them just on the point of being defrosted. This is an incredibly light meringue soufflé which is simplicity itself to make and utterly foolproof. The lack of any custard or eggy base lets the clear zingy flavour of the fruit shine through.

SERVES 4

FRUIT PURÉE:
15 passion fruits
90 g (3 oz) caster sugar
butter, for greasing
caster sugar, for coating

7 egg whites
pinch salt
6 tablespoons caster sugar
icing sugar, for dusting

1 Prepare fruit purée. Cut passion fruits in half and remove pulp with a teaspoon. Reserve pulp from two fruits.

2 Purée pulp in a blender or food processor, if you have one, for 3–4 seconds, to separate seeds from pulp. Pour into a sieve and sieve out seeds. Just sieving will do but is harder work.

3 Cook purée in a small pan with measured sugar and reduce to a thickened pulp of the consistency of custard. Allow to cool, then chill well. This part may be done early to help preparation.

4 Grease and sugar four individual soufflé dishes. Spoon pulp from one half of remaining fruits into each dish.

5 Preheat oven to 200C (400F/Gas 6) while eating your main course. The soufflés take 2–3 minutes to make and 4–5 minutes to cook, so may easily be made while someone else is clearing the table.

6 Place egg whites in a perfectly clean bowl with a pinch of salt. Whisk until they form stiff peaks.

7 Fold in half caster sugar, whisk to form stiff glossy peaks and repeat with remaining sugar.

8 Using a balloon whisk carefully and gently fold into prepared fruit purée.

9 Pile into prepared soufflé dishes. Smooth sides and tops with a palette knife, allowing mixture to stand about 5 cm (2 inch) above rims of dishes.

10 Bake in preheated oven until risen and golden in 4–5 minutes.

11 Dust with icing sugar and serve immediately.

PUDDING:
100 g (3½ oz) self-raising flour
½ level teaspoon baking powder
¼ level teaspoon bicarbonate of
soda
1 rounded tablespoon cocoa
powder
75 g (2½ oz) caster sugar
1 extra large egg
1 tablespoon golden syrup
100 ml (3½ fl oz) milk
100 ml (3½ fl oz) sunflower oil

SAUCE:
30 g (1 oz) unsalted butter
90 g (3 oz) extra bitter dark
chocolate (Meunier or Valrona)
220 ml (7 fl oz) double cream
250g (8 oz) icing sugar

BAKED chocolate pudding WITH

HOT CHOCOLATE FUDGE SAUCE

A nursery pudding – very simple, very light and impossible to resist! This is one of the most popular puddings we have ever done at The Old Vicarage. Serve with Quick Foolproof Custard (page 68).

1 Preheat oven to 150C (300F/Gas 2).

2 Grease four individual 180ml (6 fl oz) pudding tins or bowls.

3 Prepare pudding. Sieve all dry ingredients together into a mixing bowl. Make a well in centre.

4 Beat egg and pour into bowl with syrup, milk and oil. Draw dry ingredients inwards from sides of bowl and beat into liquid ingredients to make a smooth batter.

5 Pour into prepared tins or bowls and bake in preheated oven for approximately 30 minutes, until springy to touch.

6 Prepare sauce. Melt butter, chocolate and cream together in a double boiler. Sieve icing sugar and gradually beat in to form a rich, glossy sauce.

7 To serve, unmould puddings onto dessert plates and pour fudge sauce over and around bases.

For special occasions turn a nursery pudding into something stylish. Use approximately 300ml (10 fl oz) Quick Foolproof Custard (page 68) and pour round outer edges of plates. Using a wooden skewer, draw custard and fudge sauce together in swirling pattern to serve. See photograph above.

orange & pecan pudding

WITH TOFFEE SAUCE

For a winning combination of flavours serve this very light, nursery pudding with Orange Custard. Pecans are similar to walnuts but have a smoother shape and a milder flavour.

SERVES 4

PUDDING:
butter, for greasing
60 g (2 oz) pecan nuts
60 g (2 oz) self-raising flour
¼ teaspoon baking powder
pinch of salt
1 orange
120 g (4 oz) softened unsalted butter
120 g (4 oz) soft brown sugar
2 eggs

TOFFEE SAUCE:
60 g (2 oz) pecan nuts
90 g (3 oz) caster sugar
150 ml (5 fl oz) double cream
60 g (2 oz) unsalted butter

1 Preheat oven to 160C (325F/Gas 3). Lightly grease 4 individual pudding moulds.

2 Prepare pudding. Grind pecans in a blender or food processor. Mix with flour, baking powder and a pinch of salt.

3 Grate zest from orange. Place in a bowl with butter and sugar and cream together until pale and fluffy.

4 Beat eggs and gradually whisk into mixture. Gently fold in flour mixture until pudding is evenly mixed. It should have a soft, dropping consistency. Divide mixture between prepared pudding moulds. Bake in preheated oven for about 25 minutes, until puddings are well risen and firm to touch.

5 Prepare toffee sauce while puddings are baking. Blanch pecan nuts. Place in a saucepan and cover with cold water. Bring to boil then drain. Rub skins from nuts. Roughly chop blanched pecans.

6 Place sugar in a medium-sized pan with 3 tablespoons water. Heat gently until sugar is dissolved then bring to boil. Boil rapidly until syrup becomes a deep caramel colour. Quickly whisk cream and butter into caramel. The sauce will go lumpy at first but keep whisking – it will turn smooth and glossy. Stir chopped pecans into sauce.

7 Turn puddings out carefully onto serving plates. Serve with Toffee Sauce poured over and Orange Custard (see below) poured round.

orange CUSTARD

If possible, make this custard the day before it is required and chill it in the refrigerator. This allows the flavours to develop.

SERVES 4

315 ml (10 fl oz) Quick Foolproof Custard (page 68)
1 orange

Most of the flavour of citrus fruits is contained in the oil of the zest.

1 Make custard.

2 Use a small sharp knife or a potato peeler to cut four strips of zest from orange. Do not use a zester as the zest should be removed before serving – large pieces are easier to deal with! Drop zest into warm custard. Cool, then chill.

3 Heat custard gently in a saucepan and remove zest before serving.

glazed apple tarts

These French-style apple tarts are delicious served with Caramel & Calvados Sauce and Quick Foolproof Custard (page 68).

SERVES 4

125 g (5 oz) Old Vic Foolproof Pastry (page 152)

PASTRY CREAM:
300 ml (10 fl oz) single cream
half vanilla pod
2 egg yolks
1 tablespoon plain flour
⅛ teaspoon cornflour
1 level tablespoon caster sugar

TOPPING:
3 Granny Smith apples
1 tablespoon sugar
30 g (1oz) unsalted butter
1 tablespoon water
4 bay leaves
icing sugar, to dust

To bake a pastry case blind: line with foil and baking beans and bake in a preheated oven at 190/200C (375/400F/Gas 5/6) for 10 minutes. Reduce heat to 180C (350F/Gas 4) and cook for a further 15–20 minutes. Remove the foil and beans. The pastry shell should be totally cooked and lightly golden – if not quite cooked, return it to the oven for a further 5 minutes or so.

1 Preheat oven to 190C (375F/Gas 5).

2 Roll out pastry on lightly floured surface and use to line four individual fluted tart tins. Prick bases of pastry with fork and bake blind for 15 minutes in preheated oven (see under ingredients list).

3 Prepare pastry cream. Pour cream into a small pan. Split vanilla pod and scrape seeds into cream and add pod. Bring cream to boil.

4 Blend egg yolks in a bowl with flour, cornflour and sugar. Gradually whisk in hot cream. Rinse pan and return custard to it. Cook gently, stirring continuously, until thickened and flour has cooked out, leaving no dry taste.

5 Remove pan from heat and lay buttered greaseproof over surface to prevent a skin forming. Allow to cool. Spoon into pastry cases when cold.

6 Prepare topping. Peel, core and thinly slice apples.

7 Heat sugar in a small pan with butter and 1 tablespoon water until sugar is dissolved. Bring to boil. Add apple slices and cook gently for 2 or 3 minutes, until softened and coated with buttery syrup.

8 Arrange overlapping apple slices over pastry cream. Bake tarts in oven for 7 to 8 minutes, until edges of apple have taken on a deep caramelised colour.

9 Trim each bay leaf to look like an apple leaf and arrange on each tart. Dredge with icing sugar. See picture on page 6.

caramel & calvados SAUCE

This is an excellent accompaniment to Glazed Apple Tarts.

SERVES 4

60 g (2 oz) caster sugar
2 tablespoons calvados
150 ml (5 fl oz) double cream

1 Dissolve sugar in a small pan in 1 tablespoon water over a low heat. Bring to boil and boil rapidly until sugar syrup starts to turn golden and a caramel is formed.

2 Remove pan from heat and dip base in cold water briefly to cool pan and prevent caramel turning too brown. Add calvados and double cream, swirling them around pan to mix.

3 Reduce over a low heat until sauce thickens and deepens in colour.

winter

In winter we need comfort food to protect us from the weather's hard edges. This is the season of crackling log fires and warming spicy food; of comforting casseroles and roasts and the robust flavours of meaty stews. All the feathered game as well as wild rabbit, hare and deer come into their own as do flavourings like juniper, cinnamon and port. Winter food is earthy, gutsy and welcoming, with the warm intoxicating smells of long slow cooking filling the house.

This is pudding time; treacle sponge and plum pudding, mulled pears and mincemeat.

It is a time of making candies and fudge and spending time in the kitchen for recreation.

mussel AND SAFFRON soup

The basis of this delicious soup is a mussel stock which may be prepared a little in advance. Serve with Fennel Bread (page 142).

SERVES 4

MUSSEL STOCK:
20 rope-cultured mussels
1 small onion
1 small leek
1 bulb fennel
1 stick celery
2 cloves garlic
15 g (½ oz) unsalted butter
good pinch saffron stems
3 sprigs thyme
3 or 4 leaves lovage
5 or 6 peppercorns
150 ml (5 fl oz) white wine

THE SOUP:
24 rope-cultured mussels
300 ml (10 fl oz) fish stock (page 140)
300 ml (10 fl oz) double cream
mussel stock, prepared above
chopped fresh chives
chopped fennel fronds
salt and ground black pepper
2 tablespoons double cream

MUSSEL STOCK

1   Scrub mussels and pull of beards. Trim half onion, white part of leek and a small piece of fennel. Chop roughly with celery. Peel and chop garlic.

2   Melt butter in a large pan, add prepared vegetables and garlic. Cook until soft. Do not allow vegetables to brown.

3   Add saffron, herbs and peppercorns. Mix wine with 150 ml (5 fl oz) water and add to pan. Bring to boil.

4   Add cleaned mussels to pan and cook until mussels open. Shake pan over heat whilst cooking.

5   Remove mussels as they open. Scoop meat from shells. Return any liquor to stock in pan. Add a further 150 ml (5 fl oz) water to pan and return liquid to boil. Remove from heat.

6   Purée stock in a blender or food processor with about a quarter of vegetables and all cooked mussels.

7   Strain stock through a fine sieve. This is now the basis of your soup.

THE SOUP

1   Scrub mussels and pull off any beards.

2   Bring fish stock to boil in a large pan and add mussels. Cook until opened. Shake pan over heat whilst cooking. Remove mussels as they open with a slotted spoon and reserve. Return any juices to pan. Reduce stock slightly by boiling rapidly.

3   Pour cream into a large frying pan and boil until thickened and very lightly browned and caramelised. It will develop a nutty flavour.

4   Stir cream into reduced fish stock and add the mussel stock prepared above. Bring almost to boil. Stir in a handful of chopped chives and a handful of chopped fennel fronds.

5   Taste soup and season if necessary. Add cooked mussels to pan and heat through briefly – do not boil as the mussels will become tough.

6   Serve soup with a swirl of cream and warm Fennel Bread (page 142).

WATERCRESS AND oyster mushroom soup

SERVES **4**

1 medium onion
30 g (1 oz) unsalted butter
250 g (9 oz) oyster mushrooms
420 ml (15 fl oz) vegetable stock
2 bunches watercress
2 tablespoons Madeira
420 ml (15 fl oz) double cream
salt and ground black pepper

This is a very simple soup with an attractive bright green colour. The oyster mushrooms in it will give the soup a good flavour to complement the watercress, but will not darken the appearance at all. Most supermarkets sell oyster mushrooms – you can even buy growbags to cultivate your own from more progressive garden centres.

1   Peel and finely chop onion.

2   Melt half butter in a large pan, add onion and fry until soft.

3   Chop mushrooms finely. Add half to onion in pan and cook until soft.

4   Pour stock into saucepan and bring to boil.

5   Wash and trim watercress. Reserve a few leaves for garnish. Plunge watercress into boiling stock and leave for about 30 seconds, until limp and emerald green in colour. Remove pan from heat.

6   Purée soup immediately in a blender or food processor to set a bright green colour. Rinse pan. Return soup to pan, passing it through a sieve.

7   Melt remaining butter in a small pan and fry remaining chopped mushrooms. Add Madeira to pan and reduce to evaporate liquid.

8   Add cream and bring to boil. Reduce again to thicken and slightly caramelise cream, giving a nutty flavour.

9   Stir caramelised cream into watercress purée and heat gently. Season to taste with salt and pepper. Garnish with reserved watercress leaves before serving.

fillet of brill WITH A CORIANDER & CUMIN

CRUST

2 × 250 g (9 oz) fillets brill

CRUST:
1 tablespoon coriander seeds
1 tablespoon cumin seeds
1 tablespoon plain flour
salt and coarsely ground black
pepper

VEGETABLE TAGLIOLINI:
1 small carrot
1 small leek
1 small courgette
15 g (½ oz) unsalted butter
salt and ground black pepper
extra virgin olive oil, for frying

Brill, like turbot, is one of the finer flat fish found in our coastal waters. It has a very white meaty flesh which lends itself well to this robust treatment. Serve with Sherry Vinegar Sauce (see below).

1 Preheat oven to 200C (400F/Gas 6).

2 Skin brill fillets with a sharp knife and cut each in half to give four pieces.

3 Prepare crust. Grind coriander and cumin seeds roughly in a pestle and mortar or with an end of a rolling pin. In a small bowl mix seeds together with flour salt and pepper.

4 Prepare vegetables for tagliolini. They should resemble tagliolini, that is thin spaghetti. Peel carrot, use only white part of leek and trim courgette. Slice down length using a sharp knife or mandolin, then slice again into thin batons.

5 Season brill fillets. Press crust mixture onto upper side of fillets.

6 Heat a little olive oil in a heavy based frying pan. Cook fillets crust down until golden. Using a fish slice remove from pan to a baking sheet, crust side uppermost.

7 Bake brill in preheated oven for 3 or 4 minutes, until crust is crispy and fish is cooked through.

8 While brill is baking melt butter in frying pan. Stir fry prepared vegetables until just softened but still crisp. Season to taste.

9 Serve fish on a bed of vegetable tagliolini.

sherry vinegar sauce

1 cinnamon stick
1 teaspoon coriander seed
2 tablespoons amontillado sherry
1 tablespoon sherry vinegar
2 teaspoons dark soy sauce
150 ml (5 fl oz) reduced fish stock
(page 140)
125 g (4 oz) chilled unsalted
butter
salt and ground black pepper
chopped fresh coriander, to
garnish

1 Break cinnamon stick. Place in small pan with coriander seed, sherry, sherry vinegar, soy and fish stock.

2 Simmer for 5 minutes to blend flavours.

3 Whisk in small cubes of chilled butter until a smooth, thickened sauce is formed.

4 Pass sauce through a sieve into a clean pan to remove flavourings.

5 Season to taste, reheat if necessary and add chopped coriander leaf.

We serve this at The Old Vicarage with Sherry Vinegar Sauce poured round the vegetables.

FRESH canneloni WITH LEEKS, MUSHROOMS & PINE KERNELS

SERVES 4 AS A STARTER

half a quantity of Fresh Saffron Pasta (page 147)

FILLING:
2 leeks
8 mushrooms
30 g (1 oz) pine kernels
2 tablespoons extra virgin olive oil
3 sprigs thyme
freshly grated nutmeg

SAUCE:
450 ml (15 fl oz) double cream
thyme leaves
salt and ground black pepper
30 g (1 oz) Gruyère or Parmesan, grated

Serve this vegetarian pasta dish with Celery, Apple & Fresh Walnut Salad. I use half a 300 g (10 oz) pasta mixture (page 147) for this recipe for 4 people as a starter.

1 Roll out pasta thinly on a floured surface or put through a pasta machine on No.6 setting. Cut into pieces of approximately 10 × 7.5 cm (4 × 3 inch). Freeze remaining pasta for later use.

2 Moisten one edge of pasta with water and fold over to form tubes. Dry out on a broom handle for about 1 hour.

3 When pasta is dry, preheat oven to 220C (425F/Gas 7).

4 Boil a large pan of salted water. Add dry cannelloni tubes and cook for 1–2 minutes. Rinse well in cold water and pat dry.

5 Trim and finely chop leeks. Chop mushrooms. Toast pine kernels until golden, by stir frying for a minute or two in a hot, dry frypan.

6 Heat olive oil in a fry pan, add prepared vegetables and cook until soft. Add pine kernels, nutmeg and half the thyme leaves. Mix well.

7 Fill cannelloni tubes with leek mixture and arrange in an ovenproof dish.

8 Prepare sauce. Pour double cream for sauce into a pan, add the remaining thyme leaves and boil cream until slightly thickened. Season lightly.

9 Pour cream over cannelloni and top with grated cheese.

10 Bake in preheated oven for about 5 minutes, until golden. The top should be crispy with remaining pasta soft in a bubbling sauce.

11 Serve immediately. Remove cannelloni to plates using two palette knives to lift tubes and spoon a little of cream sauce round pasta.

I sometimes roll the cannelloni around a tube of plastic wrap and leave them to dry with the film inside. In this state they freeze well and can be cooked from frozen – useful for entertaining.

CELERY, APPLE & FRESH walnut salad

SERVES 4

DRESSING:
1 clove garlic
2 tablespoons extra virgin olive oil
2 teaspoons balsamic vinegar
salt and ground black pepper

(continued on next page)

Try to use new season's wet walnuts for this salad. They have pale skins and a lovely creamy texture without any hint of bitterness.

1 Prepare dressing. Leave garlic whole and place in a screw-top jar with other ingredients. Shake well to blend then leave to infuse. Remove garlic before serving dressing.

2 Shell walnuts using nutcrackers or a heavy weight.

125 g (4 oz) new season's walnuts
iced water
1 curly endive
16 rosettes lambs lettuce
golden marjoram leaves
4 sticks celery
2 eating apples

3   Blanch nuts. Place in a pan of cold water and bring to boil. Remove from heat and plunge nuts into iced water. The skins will loosen and can be peeled off.

4   Wash endive, lambs lettuce and marjoram. Use only middle of endive.

5   Trim, wash and chop celery. Core and thinly slice apples – do not peel.

6   Mix all salad ingredients together in a large bowl.

7   Remove garlic from dressing, shake well and pour over salad. Toss thoroughly to coat leaves.

hazelnut tagliatelle WITH WILD
MUSHROOMS & CASHEWS

SERVES 4

1 quantity hazelnut pasta
(page 147)
1 quantity watercress pasta
(page 147)

WILD MUSHROOM & CASHEW NUT
SAUCE:
180 g (6 oz) mixed wild
mushrooms
(girolles, shiitake and oyster
mushrooms are all readily
available in good supermarkets)
125 g (4 oz) cashew nuts
30 g (1 oz) unsalted butter
1 tablespoon Madeira
150 ml (5 fl oz) double cream
150 ml (5 fl oz) vegetable stock
chopped fresh chives
chopped fresh parsley
salt and ground black pepper

We experimented with using nuts in pasta in our quest for new vegetarian ideas. It works well provided the nuts are finely ground. The nut oil makes the pasta pliable and easy to work with.

1   Make pastas as described on page 147. Chill until required and for at least 1 hour.

2   Roll out pastas very thinly and cut into tagliatelle as described on page 147.

3   Boil a large pan of salted water. Blanch pasta for 1 minute. Drain.

4   Prepare sauce. Slice mushrooms thickly. Toast cashews under hot grill until golden.

5   Melt butter in large pan, add mushrooms and cook until just soft.

6   Add Madeira to mushrooms and reduce over a high heat until liquid is concentrated and sticky.

7   Stir in cashew nuts and double cream. Boil rapidly until thickened and slightly caramelised.

8   Toss blanched tagliatelle in sauce, adding as much vegetable stock as required to give a light sauce for pasta.

9   Add a handful of freshly chopped chives and parsley. Season to taste.

10 Serve immediately.

300 ml (10 fl oz) single cream may be used in place of double cream and vegetable stock. This dish is excellent when served with Lemon Dressed Pear & Watercress Salad (page 114).

LEMON DRESSED
pear & watercress salad

SERVES 4

1 bunch watercress
1 bunch rocket
1 dessert pear

DRESSING:
1 lemon
1 small clove garlic
4 tablespoons extra virgin olive oil
1 teaspoon caster sugar
salt and ground black pepper

1 Prepare dressing. Pare a strip of lemon zest, squeeze juice from lemon and place both in a screw-top jar.

2 Crush garlic and add to lemon juice with olive oil, sugar, salt and pepper. Shake until blended.

3 Wash and dry watercress and rocket. Peel, core and slice pear – mix with leaves in a bowl.

4 Shake dressing again and pour carefully over salad, removing lemon zest. Toss together. Serve in a pretty glass bowl or arrange on individual plates.

We serve this at The Old Vicarage with Hazelnut & Watercress Tagliatelle with Wild Mushrooms & Cashew Nuts (page 113).

sea bass COOKED WITH SESAME & FIVE SPICE

SERVES 4

FIVE SPICE MIXTURE:
1 teaspoon coriander seed
1 teaspoon Szechuan peppercorns
1 stick cinnamon
2 pieces star anise
1 clove garlic

BASS:
2 × 1 kg (2 lb) bass
1 tablespoon sesame oil
salt and ground black pepper
2 leeks
half a cucumber
8 spring onions
2–3 tablespoons white wine

SAUCE:
1 shallot
1 clove garlic
15 g (½ oz) unsalted butter
2 tablespoons red wine vinegar
150 ml (5 fl oz) fish stock
(page 140)
150 ml (5 fl oz red wine)
1 piece star anise
1 teaspoon dark soy sauce
1 teaspoon sugar
chilled unsalted butter
fresh coriander

For four people you will need two 1 kg (2 lb) bass. Ask your fishmonger to scale and fillet the fish but to leave the skin on – this is a very pretty blue and silver colour. I like to mark the skin with a hot skewer to make it look char-grilled (see page 57).

Although you can buy perfectly good Chinese Five Spice I like to make my own. Grinding your own spice mixtures is very satisfying and, I think, worth the effort.

1 Prepare spice mixture. Place coriander seed, peppercorns, cinnamon stick and 2 pieces star anise in a mortar. Peel and crush one clove garlic, adding it to spices. Grind together with a pestle.

2 Preheat oven to 200C (400F/Gas 6).

3 Rub skins of bass with sesame oil. Sprinkle flesh with five spice powder and season with salt and pepper.

4 Trim leeks and use white parts only. Scrape out and discard seeds from cucumber using a teaspoon. Cut leeks and cucumber into fine strips. Trim spring onions and slice finely.

5 Strew a baking dish with prepared vegetables. Moisten with 2 or 3 tablespoons white wine.

6 Sit bass fillets on vegetables, skin side uppermost. Bake, uncovered, in preheated oven for 4–5 minutes, until flesh is just cooked and skin is starting to catch and go crispy round the edges.

7 While fish is cooking prepare sauce. Finely chop shallot and peel and crush remaining garlic.

8 Melt butter in a small pan, add onion and garlic and cook until soft but not coloured.

9 Add red wine vinegar and boil rapidly until reduced by half. Add fish stock and red wine and reduce again by half.

10 Crush remaining star anise and add to pan with soy sauce and sugar. Simmer for 4 to 5 minutes to allow flavours to blend. Strain sauce through a sieve into a clean pan.

11 Whisk in small pieces of chilled butter over a low heat until sauce is thickened and has a glossy appearance and a deep colour. Taste the sauce and season if necessary.

12 Chop some fresh coriander leaf and stir it into sauce.

13 Serve bass, skin side up, on a bed of vegetables with sauce poured round.

WARM chicken liver mousse

WITH BACON & BAY LEAF

250 g (9oz) chicken livers
fresh milk, for soaking
1 small onion
2 rashers streaky bacon
90 g (3 oz) unsalted butter
1 clove garlic
1 bay leaf
2 sprigs thyme
1 tablespoon amontillado sherry
1 egg
150 ml (5 fl oz) double cream
salt and ground black pepper
unsalted butter, for greasing

This makes an excellent starter or a light lunch dish served hot with toast or toasted brioche, a small salad and a good spoonful of crab apple jelly.

1 Preheat oven to 140C (275F/Gas 1).

2 Remove any green parts from chicken livers and discard. Soak livers in milk to remove any trace of bitterness.

3 Use half small onion and chop it finely. Remove rinds from bacon and dice rashers.

4 Melt butter in a large frying pan. Add onion and bacon and cook until onion is soft. Peel and crush garlic and add to pan.

5 Drain chicken livers and add to pan with herbs. Fry briskly until livers are browned on outside but still pink inside. Remove livers from pan.

6 Add sherry to pan and bring to boil. Scrape up any crusty meaty bits from base of pan into liquid and simmer for a few minutes to blend flavours. Remove from heat. Cool slightly.

7 Beat egg in a small bowl with cream. Add to pan with chicken livers and season to taste.

8 Purée in a blender or food processor until smooth. Pass through a medium sieve into a clean bowl.

9 Pour into four greased dariole moulds or small, straight sided cups.

10 Line a roasting tin with two folded household cloths or muslin. Stand moulds in tin and pour in boiling water to a depth of one third of moulds. This allows mousse to cook more slowly and evenly, and also prevents it becoming granular.

11 Bake in preheated oven for about 30–40 minutes, until centre of mousses feel firm to touch.

12 Remove from oven. Run a thin knife around sides of moulds and turn out mousses onto serving plates.

13 Serve hot with toast or toasted brioche, a small salad and a good spoonful of crab apple jelly.

A large glass of chilled Alsace muscat would be the perfect accompaniment.

roast loin of pork WITH HAZELNUT

& APPLE STUFFING

SERVES 4

1.8 kg (4 lb) boned and rolled loin
of pork
2 fat cloves garlic
6 sage leaves
6 sprigs thyme
freshly ground sea salt
freshly ground black pepper
1 onion
1 carrot
1 stick celery
pork bones
1 dessertspoonful plain flour
1 glass red wine
420 ml (15 fl oz) brown chicken
stock (see page 140)

HAZELNUT & APPLE STUFFING:
60 g (2 oz) hazelnuts
1 small onion
15 g (½ oz) unsalted butter
1 Cox's Orange Pippin apple
125 g (4 oz) fresh breadcrumbs
1 tablespoon chopped fresh
thyme leaves
1 tablespoon chopped fresh
parsley
salt and ground black pepper

*Keeping the pork raised in the roasting
tin helps the skin to crackle more
easily. Leaving the skins on the
vegetables during roasting makes the
resultant sauce a richer, darker colour.*

*Serving pickled, spiced or mulled
fruits with hot or cold meats is a
peculiarly British way and one which
I think is worth preserving.*

*Ask your butcher to bone, roll and score the pork loin, and return
the bones. A very hot oven, dry skin surface and salt gives a crisp
crackling – an essential part of the appeal of this dish. We serve this
at The Old Vicarage with Pickled Plums (page 148).*

1   Preheat oven to hottest setting. Dry pork joint with absorbent kitchen
paper. Place pork on chopping board. Make incisions into flesh of
pork with point of a sharp knife – make incisions into flesh under
scored crackling as well. Cut garlic into slivers and insert with torn
sage leaves and tiny sprigs of thyme into the incisions. Rub surface of
pork with salt (ground sea salt is best) and finish with pepper. Do not
use any cooking fat – there will be enough from pork.

2   Wash and roughly chop vegetables, do not peel. Place in a roasting tin
with pork bones to form a trivet. Sit prepared pork on vegetables.

3   Roast pork in very hot preheated oven for about 30 minutes, until skin
has crackled. Reduce heat to 200C (400F/Gas 6). Roast for a further
45 minutes.

4   Prepare stuffing while pork is roasting. Roast hazelnuts (see page 152).
Chop hazelnuts and place in a bowl. Finely chop only half onion. Melt
butter in a small pan, add chopped onion and cook until softened.
Peel, core and finely dice apple.

5   Add cooked onion to hazelnuts with apple, breadcrumbs, herbs, salt
and pepper and mix well. Add sufficient boiling water to give a moist
paste which will cling together. Form stuffing into twelve little balls
and place each in a small 12 hole bun tin. Pour a teaspoon of fat from
joint being roasted over each stuffing balls. Roast in oven for 15
minutes. This will give a moist stuffing with a crisp, crusty outside.

6   Test meat by inserting a skewer – the juices should run clear. If pork is
not cooked at this stage a further 10–15 minutes should complete
cooking. Remove pork from roasting tin and leave in a warm place,
uncovered, to rest.

7   Pour excess fat from tin, leaving about 1 tablespoonful. Blend flour
into fat in tin with a wooden spoon or whisk. Place roasting tin on hob
and, over a medium heat, whisk in wine and then stock. Scrape up all
crusty bits from base of tin. Making sauce in roasting tin will also
extract maximum flavour and colour from bones and vegetables.
Season to taste. Strain sauce through a large sieve into a sauce boat,
discarding bones and vegetables.

8   Carve pork into slices and serve with stuffing balls, pieces of crackling
and sauce.

CASSEROLED shin of beef

SERVES 4

1.25–1.4 kg (2½–3 lb) piece shin of beef
salt and ground black pepper
90 g (3 oz) beef dripping
1 tablespoon sunflower oil
1 onion
1 carrot
1 leek
1 bottle full bodied red wine (eg Australian Cabernet, Spanish Rioja etc)
940 ml (30 fl oz) good beef stock (see page 141)

BOUQUET GARNI:
2 sprigs parsley
4 sprigs thyme
2 bay leaves
1 stick celery, all tied together in a bundle)

AROMATICS:
4 cloves
12 juniper berries
1 cinnamon stick, broken into pieces
20 black peppercorns
salt

chopped fresh parsley, to garnish

This makes a very elegant terrine using the same ingredients and method. Simply sieve out the vegetables and bones at the end of the cooking time and pour the remainder into a terrine dish. The gelatinous cowheel will give you a lovely natural shimmering set.

Serve the casserole hot with Pot Roasted Vegetables (page 121).

This is actually my Grandmother's recipe and I can remember her making it for me. Served as a hot casserole it is a real winter warmer.

If you can get a cow heel, blanch it, split into 4 season and brown with the beef in step 2. It adds a wonderful richness to the casserole flavour.

1   Preheat oven to 150C (300F/Gas 2).

2   Remove any thick cartilage from beef and slice meat into rounds about 2 cm (¾ inch) thick. Season with salt and pepper.

3   Heat a heavy frying pan or skillet until evenly hot. Add dripping and oil. When foaming fry beef on all sides to sear and seal in juices. This really improves flavour of meat. Remove beef using a slotted spoon.

4   Place beef in a deep casserole. Earthenware gives good cooking results. It also feels and looks rustic, which is just right for this dish.

5   Chop onion, dice carrot and trim and slice leek. Add to fat in pan and cook until golden. Add a dash of wine and let it reduce over a high heat to a sticky glaze. Add a little stock and let that reduce in same way.

6   Keep adding wine and stock alternately, repeating reducing process above, to give a good deep sauce base. Use half the wine and half the stock for this process.

7   Make bouquet garni and tuck it down amongst beef to allow flavours to slowly disperse during the long, slow cooking process.

8   Add aromatics with remaining wine and stock. Bring to boil then pour over beef in cooking pot.

9   Cover with a lid or foil and cook in centre of preheated oven for 3½ hours, or until beef is meltingly tender.

10 Remove casserole from oven. Carefully lift out beef and cow heel (if using) using a slotted spoon and keep warm. Discard the cow heel.

11 Press remaining cooking liquor and vegetables through a sieve into a clean saucepan. Press vegetables to extract all their flavour. The sauce will have reduced during cooking.

12 Season sauce with salt and pepper. Reduce over a high heat if further thickening is required.

13 Arrange beef in a serving dish and pour sauce around. Garnish with chopped fresh parsley.

POT ROASTED vegetables

1 celeriac root
3 carrots
4 leeks
12 shallots
2 parsnips
60 g (2 oz) beef dripping
1 tablespoon brown sugar
300 ml (10 fl oz) vegetable stock
1 teaspoon salt
1 bay leaf

These vegetables are an ideal accompaniment to Casseroled Shin of Beef.

1 Preheat oven to 200C (400F/Gas 6).

2 Wash and peel all vegetables. Cut them into attractive shapes, giving a variety of shapes and colours. Keep them all roughly equal in size and leave shallots whole.

3 Heat dripping in a large frying pan.

4 Fry vegetables briskly on all sides, shaking pan and stirring vegetables.

5 Sprinkle brown sugar over vegetables and allow to caramelise slightly.

6 Add stock, salt and bay leaf to pan and bring to boil. Pour into an ovenproof dish. Pot roast in preheated oven for about 20 minutes, until vegetables are cooked and have taken on a golden colour.

7 Drain vegetables from cooking liquor and serve.

BRAISED red cabbage

SERVES 4

1 small red cabbage
1 large onion
3 Cox's apples
4 tablespoons extra virgin olive oil
2 tablespoons amontillado sherry
2 tablespoons red wine vinegar
3 level tablespoons brown sugar
grated fresh nutmeg
2 cinnamon sticks, broken into pieces
salt and ground black pepper

This is a very easy going dish which can be made in advance and reheated. It will keep warm without any harm, so is very useful for entertaining. I have also frozen it successfully.

1 Cut cabbage in half and remove middle core with a sharp knife. Make a chiffonade, that is, finely shred leaves.

2 Chop onion finely. Peel, core and dice apples.

3 Place onion and olive oil in a saucepan, cook until onion is soft. Add diced apple, then shredded cabbage.

4 Add sherry and wine vinegar. Reduce slightly.

5 Stir sugar in until dissolved, then add nutmeg, cinnamon, salt and pepper.

6 Cover and simmer gently for 90 minutes or until flavours have blended and cabbage is soft. Most liquid will evaporate leaving a syrupy aromatic residue around cabbage.

7 Check seasoning, remove cinnamon and serve.

1.4 kg (3 lb) monkfish tail
salt and ground black pepper
3 lemons
3 fat cloves garlic
8 tablespoons chopped fresh
parsley
125 g (4 oz) fresh brown
breadcrumbs
3 tablespoons extra virgin olive oil
680 g (1½ lb) small spinach leaves
extra virgin olive oil, for frying

MEDALLIONS OF roast monkfish TAIL

WITH A PROVENCALE CRUST

1 Preheat oven to 200C (400F/Gas 6).

2 Cut and remove 'flappy bits' from monkfish tail and all blue skin.

3 Using a very sharp knife and with tail bone to guide knife blade, cut
down either side of tail bone and remove both fillets of monkfish.
Carefully trim fillets of all skin – this toughens during cooking.

4 Wash fish and pat dry. Season with salt and pepper.

5 Remove zest from lemons with a zester or fine grater. Peel and finely
chop garlic. Mix lemon zest, chopped garlic, parsley and breadcrumbs
together in a small bowl and add olive oil, stirring until crumbs just
bind together.

6 Coat monkfish fillets with crumb mixture, pressing it firmly onto fish.
Place crumbed fillets on a baking sheet or in a shallow roasting tin.

7 Roast in preheated oven for 6 or 8 minutes, until fish feels firm and
crumbs are crispy and golden. Rest fish in a warm place for a few
minutes.

8 Wash spinach leaves thoroughly while fish is cooking and shake dry.
Heat a little olive oil in a large frying pan and quickly stir fry spinach
for about 1 minute. Season to taste with salt and pepper.

Try serving this with Tomato &
Chilli Salsa (page 150) as we do at
The Old Vicarage.

9 Slice monkfish fillets carefully to form round medal shapes with a
crispy topping. Lay overlapping slices on a bed of spinach and serve
with Tomato & Chilli Salsa (page 150).

POT ROASTED pheasant WRAPPED IN PANCETTA

SERVES 4

2 tablespoons pitted green olives
salt and ground black pepper
1 brace oven-ready pheasants
a few sprigs thyme
60 g (2 oz) unsalted butter
1 pig's trotter, cut into four
1 onion
1 small celeriac
1 bottle red wine (a Rhône would be excellent)
150 ml (5 fl oz) amontillado sherry
2 fresh bay leaves
1 cinnamon stick, broken into pieces
6 thin slices pancetta or streaky bacon, rind removed

This is delicious served with Mashed Potatoes with Olive Oil (page 144). Ask the butcher to cut the pig's trotter into four pieces for you.

1   Preheat oven to 200C (400F/Gas 6). Soak olives in water to remove saltiness.

2   Season pheasants. Insert a few tiny sprigs of thyme into the breast using the point of a small knife. Melt butter in a large frying pan and sear pheasants on all sides. Remove pheasants from pan and set to one side.

3   Sear pig's trotter pieces in pan. Chop onion and celeriac and add to pan. Brown slightly with trotter.

4   Add red wine and sherry to pan and bring to boil. Cook for 10 minutes to drive off alcohol.

5   Pour contents of pan into a roasting tin. Drain olives and rinse. Add olives to roasting tin with bay leaves and cinnamon stick. Place pheasants on top of trotters and vegetables, breast side down, and roast in preheated oven for 25 minutes.

6   Remove roasting tin from oven. Sit pheasant breast side up and cover breasts with pancetta or bacon rashers with rinds removed. Baste well.

7   Return pheasants to oven to complete cooking. This will take between 20 minutes for younger birds and 50 minutes for much older birds. Test by inserting a skewer in thickest part of thigh – juices should run clear when pheasants are cooked through. Remove cinnamon stick and bay leaves.

8   Remove pheasants, trotter and olives and keep warm. Place roasting tin on hob and reduce juices by boiling if necessary. Press sauce through a sieve into a clean pan. Heat gently while whisking to give a rich, gelatinous sauce. Season if necessary.

9   Remove breasts by cutting down either side of the breast bones and working the knife along the rib cage. Cut off legs and thighs at hip joints. Serve a breast and a leg to each person with a piece of trotter, Mashed Potatoes with Olive Oil and a good dollop of crab apple jelly.

roast english partridge

ON BUTTERY CELERIAC STICKS

4 oven-ready partridge
90 g (3 oz) softened unsalted butter
4 sprigs thyme
salt and ground black pepper

STUFFING
2 shallots
2 sticks celery with leaves
4 bay leaves
small wine glass sherry
1 small celeriac
300 ml (10 fl oz) brown chicken stock (page 140)
60 g (2 oz) chilled unsalted butter

I find that English Greyleg partridge have the finest flavour – it is worth asking for them by name. This makes an excellent meal when served with Bubble & Squeak (page 145) and Game Liver Crostini (page 124).

1   Preheat oven to 220C (425F/Gas 7).

2   Lift skin on partridge breasts with your fingers and smear a little of the softened butter over breasts. Add a few thyme leaves for seasoning under breast skin. Season partridges inside and out with salt and pepper.

3   Prepare stuffing. Peel and finely chop shallots. Finely chop celery and leaves. Place shallots, celery and bay leaves inside partridges.

4   Heat remaining butter in a large frying pan or skillet and sear partridges on all sides to seal. Transfer partridges to a roasting tin. Do not wash the pan.

5   Pour a small wine glass of sherry over birds then roast in preheated oven for 10 minutes. Remove from oven.

6   While partridges are roasting peel celeriac and chop into batons or matchsticks.

7   Using a sharp knife cut down either side of breast bones and remove eight partridge breasts. Set to one side to rest. The breasts should be pink. Rest in a warming oven. Reserve the bones for stock.

8   Remove legs from partridges, including fleshy thighs, and return to oven in roasting tin to finish roasting. This will take a further 10–15 minutes. Test thighs by inserting a skewer – meat should be tender and juices should run clear. Baste frequently so skin becomes dark brown and sticky. Reserve partridge carcasses for stock.

9   While thighs are roasting prepare a sauce. Add reserved breast bones and partridge carcasses to the large frying pan or skillet. Heat over a high heat to brown and add chicken stock. Reduce to give a good flavour and sieve. Whisk a few knobs of chilled butter into finished sauce to thicken and give a glossy appearance.

10 Melt a little butter in a small frypan and cook celeriac batons until just softened. Season to taste. Slice partridge breasts.

11 Serve partridge breasts on celeriac. Put a small patty of Bubble & Squeak (page 145) on each plate and prop roast partridge legs against it.

The roast partridge legs are quite delectable finger food. Don't forget to have finger bowls at the ready.

FAR RIGHT
Pot roasted pheasant wrapped in pancetta (recipe page 124).

RIGHT
Roast English partridge on buttery celeriac sticks (recipe page 125) with Bubble and Squeak and game liver crostini.

game liver crostini

This is a good way of using up the livers from game birds.

SERVES 4

1 dessertspoon pine kernels
1 French stick
1 clove garlic
extra virgin olive oil
livers from four game birds, partridges, pheasants etc
salt and ground black pepper
30 g (1 oz) unsalted butter
2 tablespoons amontillado sherry
chopped fresh parsley

1   Toast pine kernels under hot grill or in a hot, dry frypan until golden. Set to one side.

2   Cut four slices from French stick. Cut garlic clove and rub over surface of sliced bread. Heat some olive oil in a large frying pan. Fry bread until crisp and golden. Remove from pan and drain on absorbent kitchen paper.

3   Trim livers (make sure bile sac has been removed). Season with salt and pepper. Add butter to oil in pan, and heat until melted. Fry livers briskly on all sides until cooked but still pink in middle. Add toasted pine kernels and sherry and heat for a few seconds, scraping any crusty juices up into sherry.

4   Pile livers onto garlic crostini. Spoon cooking juices over and top with chopped parsley or pine kernels. Serve immediately.

Serve with any roast game birds.

OLD VIC GRILLED cheese savoury WITH

ANCHOVIES & GARLIC

SERVES 4

2 shallots
1 fat clove garlic
7 g (¼ oz) unsalted butter
2 eggs
2 tablespoons double cream
1 tablespoon whole grain mustard
180 g (6 oz) mature Cheddar
cheese
4 small bread rolls
12 marinated anchovy fillets
4 black olives
4 sprigs parsley

This could happily replace the traditional cheese course in a meal. Serve after the main dish, to help finish the wine in a continental manner or, in more traditional British style, serve at the end of your meal topped with bacon curls or Devils on Horseback.

1   Peel and finely chop shallots. Peel and crush garlic.

2   Melt butter in a small pan, add shallot and garlic and cook slowly to soften. Do not allow vegetables to colour.

3   Beat eggs and cream together with a fork in a small bowl. Grate cheese. Add egg mixture to pan off the heat and stir in mustard and grated cheese. Continue stirring until thoroughly mixed.

4   Cook over low heat, stirring constantly, until mixture thickens and amalgamates. Treat it as you would lightly scrambled egg. Remove from heat, tip into a bowl and allow to cool.

5   Preheat grill.

6   Split rolls and toast. Pile the cheese savoury onto the cut surfaces and toast again until golden and puffed up.

7   Slice anchovies in half lengthways. Cut olives in half and remove stones.

8   Top savouries with anchovies and olives. Return to grill to warm garnish then decorate with sprigs of parsley and serve immediately.

A little dressed salad makes a good accompaniment. The same mixture served on small croûtes is perfect as a drinks party savoury.

PINEAPPLE, BANANA & RUM filo

SERVES 4

2 medium bananas
1 small pineapple
30 g (1 oz) shelled pistachio nuts
60 g (2 oz) ground almonds
2 tablespoons brown sugar
4 tablespoons dark rum
60 g (2 oz) unsalted butter
4 large sheets filo pastry
icing sugar, to dredge

Serve with Chocolate Rum Sauce . For special effect you could serve with Almond Tuilles (page 153) and a scoop of Vanilla Ice Cream.

Make the filling for this dessert the night before, or earlier in the day, to allow the flavours to develop.

1 Peel and slice bananas. Peel and core pineapple. Cut flesh into small cubes. Mix fruits, nuts, sugar and rum together in a bowl. Cover and leave for several hours, or overnight, to allow flavours to develop.

2 Preheat oven to 220C (425F/Gas 7).

3 Melt butter and brush over 2 sheets filo pastry. Top with remaining pastry and brush again. Cut each set of pastry in half to make four pieces of double thickness.

4 Drain any liquid from fruits and divide mixture between four sheets of pastry. Fold two long sides of pastry over filling and roll up, totally enclosing fruit.

5 Place filo rolls on a baking sheet, brush with remaining butter and dredge with icing sugar.

6 Bake in preheated oven for 12–15 minutes, until crisp and golden brown. Dredge with icing sugar to serve.

chocolate rum SAUCE

SERVES 4

30 g (1 oz) unsalted butter
125 g (4 oz) dark bitter chocolate
220 ml (7 fl oz) double cream
60 ml (2 fl oz) rum
180 g (6 oz) icing sugar

This makes the perfect accompaniment to Pineapple, Banana & Rum Filo.

1 Place butter, chocolate and cream together in a double boiler or a bowl over a pan of warm water. Heat until melted.

2 Add rum. Sieve icing sugar and gradually beat into sauce.

3 Remove from heat. Taste and add more rum if necessary. The sauce will be dark and glossy. Serve warm.

BITTER CHOCOLATE truffle cake WITH
TWO SAUCES

CHOCOLATE SPONGE:
4 eggs
180 g (6 oz) caster sugar
60 g (2 oz) cocoa powder
60 g (2 oz) cornflour
60 ml (2 fl oz) rum

CHOCOLATE TRUFFLE:
600 ml (1 pint) double cream
450g (1 lb) good bitter dark chocolate

STRAWBERRY COULIS:
375 g (12 oz) strawberries
150 g (5 oz) caster sugar
150 ml (5 fl oz) water
1 lemon

BITTER CHOCOLATE SAUCE:
100 g (4 oz) good bitter dark chocolate
¼ tsp ground cinnamon
125 ml (5 fl oz) water
50 g (2 oz) melted unsalted butter

Chocoholics everywhere – this is your cake! Dark, smooth and very rich. Use the best chocolate you can buy – I like couverture. Look for at least 50% cocoa solids.

1 Preheat oven to 200C (400F/Gas 6). Grease and line a large Swiss roll tin about 30 cm × 20 cm (12 inch × 8 inch).

2 Whisk eggs and 125 g (4 oz) sugar together in a large bowl until light and fluffy. The mixture will leave a thick trail when it is ready.

3 Sieve together cocoa and cornflour and fold into eggs – do this lightly, so as not to break down volume and make sponge heavy.

4 Pour mixture into prepared tin and bake in preheated oven for 7–8 minutes, until firm and springy. Turn out onto a wire rack and cool.

5 Cut two circles from sponge to fit base of a deep 20 cm (8 inch) round cake tin. Use one now and freeze one for next time.

6 Heat rum and remaining sugar with 60 ml (2 fl oz) water in a small saucepan until sugar is dissolved. Bring to boil and reduce to a heavy syrup. Brush rum syrup over sponge, place in base of cake tin and set to one side.

7 Prepare chocolate truffle. Stand cream in a warm place. Grate chocolate on a coarse grater. Melt chocolate very gently in a double boiler. Do not allow water to boil as chocolate will become grainy. Cool slightly.

8 Whisk cream to a light, floppy consistency. Gradually fold cream into chocolate using a balloon whisk.

9 Pour chocolate truffle over sponge in base of cake tin. Smooth top and leave in refrigerator to set – this will take 4 or 5 hours.

10 Prepare strawberry coulis. Remove green hulls from strawberries. Place sugar and water in small pan and heat slowly until sugar is dissolved. Simmer for about 10 minutes to make a syrup.

11 Squeeze juice from lemon and add to syrup with strawberries. Purée until smooth in a blender or food processor. Sieve coulis to remove any seeds. Chill until required.

12 Prepare chocolate sauce. Melt chocolate in a double boiler or over a pan of hot water. Gradually beat in cinnamon, water and melted butter to form a rich, glossy sauce.

13 Remove cake from tin. Dust surface with thick layer of cocoa or cover with thin layer of melted chocolate. Mark latter into portions whilst still warm.

14 Serve Chocolate Truffle Cake sliced with two sauces poured over.

PREVIOUS PAGES
130 Pineapple, banana, and rumfilo
131 Bitter chocolate truffle cake
131 Dark chocolate roulade with cognac and coffee cream

DARK chocolate roulade WITH

COGNAC & COFFEE CREAM

SERVES 4

ROULADE:
**100 g (4 oz) good quality
chocolate
4 eggs
pinch salt
100 g (4 oz) caster sugar
caster sugar, to dredge**

COFFEE CREAM:
**300 ml (10 fl oz) double cream
3 tablespoons cognac
1 tablespoon coffee essence
1 tablespoon icing sugar
icing sugar, to dredge**

*A delicate sponge with no flour content. Devastatingly rich to eat,
and simplicity itself to make.*

1 Preheat oven to 180C (350F/Gas 4). Line a Swiss roll tin with baking parchment. Cut 2 extra pieces the same size as the tin.

2 Prepare the roulade. Break chocolate into small pieces and melt in a double boiler or a bowl over hot water. Do not allow water to boil as this will make chocolate grainy. Allow chocolate to cool slightly.

3 Separate eggs, placing yolks in a medium sized bowl with sugar. Whisk until pale, thick and fluffy in texture, when mixture leaves a trail on surface.

4 Gently blend melted chocolate into mixture using a whisk or spatula.

5 Whisk egg whites in a large bowl with a pinch of salt until stiff. The salt will increase and stabilise the volume.

6 Gently fold egg whites into chocolate mixture using a balloon whisk. Pour mixture into prepared tin and allow it to find it's own level. Do not spread it out – this will knock out air and break down volume.

7 Bake in centre of preheated oven for 10–12 minutes, until firm, springy and lightly crusty.

8 Place a piece of baking parchment on the work surface and dredge with caster sugar. Turn sponge out onto prepared paper, removing paper from base of cake. Trim long edges of sponge with sharp knife.

9 Turn sponge with short edge towards you. Make an incision 1 cm (½ inch) from edge. Cover sponge with second sheet baking parchment and roll up, with parchment inside. Leave to cool on wire rack.

10 Prepare the coffee cream. Whisk double cream with cognac, coffee essence and icing sugar until thick.

11 When roulade is quite cold, gently unroll and remove inner parchment. Spread thickly with cognac cream.

12 Carefully roll roulade and place on a serving plate. Dredge with icing sugar before serving.

*Vary the amounts of coffee, cognac
and sugar in cream filling according
to taste.*

treacle sponge

WITH ORANGE SYRUP SAUCE

SERVES 4

butter, to grease moulds
caster sugar, to dust moulds
ground almonds, to dust moulds

TREACLE SPONGE:
1 orange
100 g (4 oz) softened unsalted butter
100 g (4 oz) caster sugar
1 large egg
100 g (4 oz) self raising flour
½ level teaspoonful baking powder
pinch of salt
2 tablespoons golden syrup

ORANGE SYRUP SAUCE:
1 orange
1 tablespoon sugar
3 tablespoons golden syrup

School treacle pudding was never like this – at least, not as I remember it! For best results, make certain that all ingredients are warm before you start to cook. I oven bake the puddings in individual moulds.

1   Preheat oven to 160C (325F/Gas 3). Lightly grease four individual pudding moulds and dredge each with caster sugar and ground almonds. Tap out any excess.

2   Prepare treacle sponge. Finely grate zest from orange. Cream butter, sugar and half the zest of orange in a large bowl until pale and fluffy.

3   Beat egg and add gradually to butter, beating well after each addition.

4   Mix together flour, baking powder and salt. Gently fold into bowl, using a balloon whisk or tablespoon. The mixture should have a very soft, dropping consistency.

5   Mix 2 tablespoons golden syrup with the remaining grated zest of orange. Divide between prepared moulds. Top with sponge mixture, tapping tins lightly on work surface on settle mixture evenly and to avoid air bubbles.

6   Bake for 15–20 minutes in preheated oven until well risen and golden. Mixture should feel as firm in middle as it does at edges and should have shrunk away slightly from sides of tins.

7   While puddings are baking, prepare an orange syrup sauce. Grate zest and squeeze juice from orange and place in a small pan. Add 1 tablespoon sugar and bring to boil, reducing over a high heat until concentrated in volume and flavour. Stir in golden syrup.

8   Turn puddings out onto individual plates and serve hot with syrup sauce poured round.

Serve with 300 ml (10 fl oz) Quick Foolproof Custard (page 68).

pear shortcake

SERVES 4

SHORTCAKE:
60 g (2 oz) unsalted butter
30 g (1 oz) caster sugar
60 g (2 oz) plain flour
30 g (1 oz) semolina
caster sugar, to dredge
2 William pears
icing sugar, to dredge
4 small bay leaves, optional

Pears marry very well with caramel and butterscotch flavours, so we serve this shortbread with Butterscotch Sauce and spun sugar.

1   Cut a pear template out of card.

2   Prepare shortcake. Cream butter and sugar together in a bowl until pale and fluffy. Mix flour and semolina together and gradually work into butter. Finally bind mixture together with palm of your hand – the warmth blends flour with butter.

3   Knead until smooth on a lightly floured surface. Chill for about 30 minutes.

4   Preheat oven to 150C (300F/Gas 2). Roll out shortbread on a lightly floured surface until 5 mm (¼ inch) thick. Use template and cut out 4 pear shapes. Place on a baking sheet and prick all over with a fork. Bake in preheated oven for 10–12 minutes, until very faintly coloured.

5   Lift shortbreads carefully onto a wire rack and dredge with caster sugar. Leave to cool – shortbreads will not become crisp until quite cold.

6   Choose firm, ripe pears. Cut in half length ways, then peel and remove cores.

7   Place pears cut side down on a chopping board and carefully cut slices the length of the fruit, leaving stem end intact. Press down gently with flat of your hand to fan out slices.

Become a plumbers mate! An ordinary builder's or plumber's butane gas powered blow torch has a controllable directional heat which can caramelise sugar in seconds. It gives a wonderful finish to sweet and savoury dishes

Caramel Ice Cream (page 154) goes well with this dessert.

8   Dredge pears generously with icing sugar. Preheat grill and heat pears to caramelise edges. Alternatively, using a blow torch, direct flame onto cut edges of pears to caramelise and give a deep golden colour (see below).

9   Sit pears on shortbreads and serve with Butterscotch Sauce poured round. A small bay leaf at stalk end of pears looks good.

butterscotch SAUCE

SERVES 4

60 g (2 oz) caster sugar
1 tablespoon brandy
150 ml (5 fl oz) double cream
90 g (3 oz) unsalted butter
natural vanilla essence

1   Heat sugar with 2 tablespoons water in a small pan until dissolved. Bring to boil and boil rapidly until sugar syrup turns golden and forms a caramel.

2   Quickly whisk in brandy, cream, butter and vanilla essence and keep whisking over a low heat until a smooth, golden, buttery sauce is made. Serve warm.

TESSA'S christmas pudding

MAKES 6 × I KG (2 LB) PUDDINGS

125 g (4 oz) black treacle
750 g (1½ lb) unsalted butter
750 g (1½ lb) dark muscavado
sugar
6 large eggs

180 g (6 oz) self raising flour
1 teaspoon mixed spice
1 teaspoon grated fresh nutmeg
1 teaspoon ground cinnamon

450 g (1 lb) fresh brown
breadcrumbs
1 tablespoon ground almonds
1 tablespoon good quality cocoa
powder

1 dessert apple
125 g (4 oz) dates
180 g (6 oz) walnuts
125 g (4 oz) glacé cherries
125 g (4 oz) pitted prunes
1 lemon
625 g (1¼ lb) currants
625 g (1¼ lb) sultanas
625 g (1¼ lb) raisins
125 g (4 oz) chopped mixed peel

1 wine glass rum
1 wine glass brandy
300 ml (10 fl oz) brown ale
300 ml (10 fl oz) milk

warm brandy, for flaming

Large Christmas Puddings will require 2–2¼ hours reheating time to steam, or 45–50 minutes in the oven. Do not microwave large puddings as they tend to collapse before they are heated through.

This pudding is very easy to make, rich yet light. We serve it at The Old Vicarage with a sharp strawberry coulis to cut through the richness, as well as the more traditional brandy cream.

1 Warm black treacle to make it easier to manage. Place the opened tin in a warm oven whilst weighing out remaining ingredients.

2 Place butter and sugar in a bowl and cream together until light and fluffy. Beat eggs in a small bowl. Mix together flour, mixed spice, nutmeg and cinnamon. Gradually beat eggs into mixture, alternating with flour and spice mixture.

3 Add breadcrumbs, almonds and cocoa powder.

4 Peel and grate apple. Chop dates, walnuts, cherries and prunes. Grate rind from lemon, squeeze juice.

5 Add apple, dates, walnuts, cherries, prunes, currants, sultanas, raisins and chopped mixed peel to the bowl. Mix thoroughly.

6 Add the rum, brandy, brown ale and milk and don't forget to make your wish as you stir. Cover bowl and leave in a cool place for a day to mature.

To steam: pack mixture into pudding basins and cover with greaseproof paper and foil. Steam puddings for 3 hours in a pan of simmering water.

To oven bake: preheat oven to 140C (275F/Gas 1). Lay several folded household cloths or muslins in the base of a roasting tin and stand filled pudding basins on top. Pour in sufficient boiling water to come a quarter of the way up the basins. Cover roasting tin with foil to enclose everything. Bake in preheated oven for 1–1¼ hours, until puddings are risen and firm to the touch in centre. Leave until cold or overnight.

Unmould puddings by giving basins one good shake and turning pudding out onto the palm of your hand. Cover in plastic wrap or foil and store in a cool place until Christmas Day.

To reheat: unrap pudding and place on a baking sheet in a medium hot oven at 200C (400F/Gas 6) for 20–25 minutes, or in a microwave at full power for 2–4 minutes. Exact microwave timing will depend on your oven – let them stand for 2–3 minutes before serving if microwaved. The puddings may also be returned to their basins, covered and steamed – this will take about 1¼ hours.

Pour warm brandy over puddings. Ignite with a match and serve.

basics

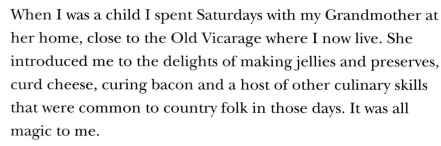

introduction

When I was a child I spent Saturdays with my Grandmother at her home, close to the Old Vicarage where I now live. She introduced me to the delights of making jellies and preserves, curd cheese, curing bacon and a host of other culinary skills that were common to country folk in those days. It was all magic to me.

One of the most valuable lessons that I learned from my grandmother was good housekeeping and being thrifty. It is much cheaper, and quite easy, to organise your forward preparations on a rolling meal basis. This means that some surplus ingredients or trimmings from one meal might form the basis of the next. Try to plan ahead.

Get into the habit of making stock on a regular basis, using trimmings, carcasses and vegetable peelings. Stock freezes well, giving you a constant ready supply. The simple sauces which are so fashionable today require only the deglazed pan juices and a little stock as the main ingredients.

Buy the very best quality ingredients that you can, only ever buy on quality – never on price. It is better to have the very best of something modest than a poor example of a supposedly finer ingredient.

To get the best quality meat or fish seek the advice of a proper independent butchers, a good traditional fishmonger and a licensed game dealer. Discuss your cooking with them; once they see that you believe in them they will try to find the very best produce for you. If you have access to independant specialists, cottage producers and traditional country markets try to use them whenever you can. Stock your store cupboard properly so that you do not need to shop for every ingredient when you are trying out a new dish. You cannot experiment unless it is all there to play with.

A good olive oil is a must. I have cold pressed extra virgin olive oil for general use. A single estate oil is a luxury and good to use in salad dressings. Search out leaf gelatine. It has a very long shelf life, is easier to use than powder and gives a real shimmer to jellies.

I would consider the following aromatics essential in a well-stocked kitchen: cinnamon sticks, cardamom pods, cloves, coriander seed, cumin seed, allspice berries, juniper berries, star anise, whole nutmegs, caraway seeds, pink peppercorns and, of course, sea salt and black peppercorns.

Fresh herbs are indispensable to all who cook. To my mind it is better to use a different fresh herb to the one specified than to use dried.

The recipes that follow are recipes I turn to again and again. Some of them are fundamental – like my Old Vic Shortcrust Pastry – others are lovely preserves that are satisfying to cook and good to have in the cupboard. Some are accompaniments to the main recipes in this book. Cook them and enjoy them.

stocks

'It is on good stock or first good broth and sauce, that excellence in cookery depends.'

ISABELLA BEETON

MAKING stocks is simply good housekeeping. The stock pot is not a repository for rubbish. However meat trimmings and, in many cases, the leftovers from vegetable preparation can all be used for flavour at no additional cost at all to you. Well made stocks are important if you are to have full-flavoured sauces.

To make a dark stock leave the skins on onions and carrots. The natural pigment present in the skins will darken the liquid. A handful of mushrooms has a similar colouring effect.

I lightly salt bones and meat trimmings before roasting – this draws out the juices. You will notice globules of solidified protein on the roasted bones. Do not salt the liquor before reducing it to the required strength; the resulting liquid would almost certainly be too salty to use.

Get into the habit of making your bones and trimmings into stock on a rolling basis so that you always have a ready supply to hand. Make a smaller amount if you only have a few bones. Fresh stocks can be kept for several days in the refrigerator or, after reducing, for up to 2 months in the freezer. Always freeze in sealed and labelled containers in usable amounts.

fish STOCK

This is probably the quickest stock to prepare because it needs so little cooking. In fact, cook it too long and you will ruin it, developing a gluey taste.

MAKES ABOUT 2.2 LITRES (3½ PINTS)

1 leek
1 large onion
1 stick celery
1 small bulb fennel
1 kg (2 lb 4 oz) fish bones and trimmings
1 bay leaf
3 or 4 parsley stalks
2 pieces star anise
1 sprig thyme
1 dessertspoon black peppercorns

1   Trim the leek and use the white part only. Chop it finely with other vegetables. Place all ingredients in a large pan and cover with cold water (about 2.5 litres or 4 pints).

2   Bring slowly to boil. Skim off any scum which floats to the surface. Reduce the heat so that stock simmers very slowly uncovered.

3   Remove from the heat and allow the stock to cool. Strain through a very fine sieve when cold. Reserve some stock in the refrigerator for immediate use. Reduce the remainder by half by fast boiling and allow it to cool. Freeze in small amounts for use as required.

Don't cover the pan during cooking – this gives a muddy, stewed taste to any stock. Fish stock will keep about 1 month in the freezer.

BASIC brown chicken
STOCK

MAKES ABOUT 2.2 LITRES (3½ PINTS)

2 raw chicken carcasses plus necks and giblets
salt
45 g (1½ oz) butter
1 leek
2 onions
2 carrots
2 sticks celery
2 glasses red wine
1 teaspoon black peppercorns
6 juniper berries
3 sprigs thyme
1 bay leaf
a few stalks parsley

1   Preheat oven to 200C (400F/Gas 6). Place carcasses, necks and giblets in a roasting tin. Salt lightly and smear with a little of the butter. Roast for 20 minutes.

2   Trim leek and chop white part only. Chop onions, carrots and celery – do not peel. Melt remaining butter in a large pan and cook vegetables until golden. Add bones.

3   Pour wine into roasting tin and cook to a sticky glaze, stirring well to scrape up any residue in tin into liquid. Add to pan with seasonings.

4   Add about 2.5 litres or 4 pints cold water, and bring to boil. Skim off any residue. Simmer slowly for 2–2½ hours, uncovered.

5   Allow to cool, then strain through a fine sieve.

beef STOCK

MAKES ABOUT 2.2 LITRES (3½ PINTS)

1.4 kg (3 lb) beef bones plus meat
trimmings
1 leek
2 onions
2 carrots
1 stick celery
1 piece celeriac
6 open mushrooms
30 g (1 oz) beef dripping or butter
1 bottle red wine
1 tablespoon black peppercorns
2 or 3 cloves
cinnamon stick
2 bay leaves
2 sprigs thyme
4 sprigs parsley
water to cover

Follow Basic Method as for
Brown Chicken Stock.

pork STOCK

MAKES ABOUT 2.2 LITRES (3½ PINTS)

1.4 kg (3 lb) pork bones and
trimmings
1 pigs trotter
1 leek
2 onions
2 carrots
2 sticks celery
30 g (1 oz) pork dripping or butter
half a bottle red wine
2.3 litres (4 pints) water
6 juniper berries
1 dessertspoon black peppercorns
2 sprigs sage
2 bay leaves
4 sprigs parsley

Follow Basic Method as for
Brown Chicken Stock.

lamb STOCK

MAKES ABOUT 2.2 LITRES (3½ PINTS)

1.8 kg (4 lb) lamb bones and
trimmings
2 leeks
2 onions
2 carrots
2 sticks celery
2 whole cloves garlic
30 g (1 oz) lamb dripping or butter
half a bottle red wine
2.3 litres (4 pints) water
1 stem rosemary
1 dessertspoon black peppercorns
2 bay leaves

Follow Basic Method as for
Brown Chicken Stock. Remove
rosemary after 1 hour. The garlic
cloves will sweeten the stock and
accentuate the lamb flavour.

white chicken STOCK

MAKES ABOUT 2.2 LITRES (3½ PINTS)

1 leek
2 onions
2 carrots
2 sticks celery
30 g (1 oz) butter
2 raw chicken carcasses plus necks
and giblets
1 teaspoon black peppercorns
3 sprigs thyme
2 bay leaves
a few parsley stalks

Follow Basic Method as for
Brown Chicken Stock but do not
pre-cook the chicken carcasses.

*This is a very versatile stock to use in
light coloured dishes. Do not add
chicken livers to stock as these may be
cooked and used in their own right.*

vegetable STOCK

*A good vegetable stock is
necessary for vegetarian cookery,
certain sauces and for soups.*

MAKES ABOUT 2.2 LITRES (3½ PINTS)

2 leeks
2 onions
2 carrots
2 sticks celery
½ small celeriac
30 g (1 oz) butter
2.3 litres (4 pints) water
1 dessertspoon black peppercorns
1 bay leaf
2 sprigs thyme
2 or 3 parsley stalks

1   Trim leek and use white part
only. Chop roughly. Wash, peel
and chop vegetables.

2   Melt butter in a large pan.
When foaming, add all prepared
vegetables and stir well, coating
them in butter. Cook until butter
is absorbed. Add a little water,
keeping heat high and stirring
until it too has been absorbed.
Add remaining water.

3   Bring to boil. Reduce heat
and cook at a fairly brisk simmer
for about 20 minutes.

4   Allow vegetables to go cold in
stock. Strain through a fine sieve.
Refrigerate for up to 5 days, or
reduce by half and freeze in
small amounts for up to 2
months.

duck STOCK

*Follow Basic Method as for
Brown Chicken Stock using duck
carcasses*

granary BREAD

The bread is cooked when it is brown on top, brown and dry on the underside and sounds hollow when tapped underneath. It should also feel light.

MAKES 48 ROLLS OR 2 LARGE LOAVES

1 kg (2 lb) bag malted Granary flour
500 g (1 lb) strong white plain flour
1 tablespoon salt
2 tablespoons brown sugar
90 g (3 oz) fresh yeast
3 tablespoons sunflower oil
800 ml (1½ pints) warm water

BASIC METHOD

1   Mix flours, salt and sugar together with your hands in a large bowl to warm them.

2   Crumble yeast. Add to flour and rub in as if making pastry. This also helps to keep everything warm.

3   Stir in oil. Gradually add warm water, making sure that you collect up any dry mixture from bottom of bowl into dough mass. Add a little extra water if necessary.

4   Knead in an electric mixer using a dough hook, at low speed, for 20 minutes. To knead by hand, turn dough onto a lightly floured surface. Pull dough with a stretching movement from outer edges to middle, giving a quarter turn each time. You will be doing this for 30 minutes, so have some beautiful thoughts ready to think!

5   Cover and leave to rise in a warm kitchen or the airing cupboard until doubled in size. This will take about 30 minutes.

6   Turn out onto a floured surface and knead lightly by hand – this is called 'knocking back'.

7   Shape into rolls and place on a lightly greased floured baking sheet, or use to fill two 750 g (1½ lb) loaf tins. Leave in a warm place for a further 20–30 minutes until risen.

8   Preheat oven to 220C (425F/Gas 7) while dough is rising.

9   Brush rolls or loaves with beaten egg and sprinkle with poppy seeds or sesame seeds.

10   Place bread in preheated oven and reduce temperature to 200C (400F/Gas 6). Bake rolls for 10–12 minutes and loaves for approximately 35–40 minutes.

11   Cool on a wire rack.

fennel BREAD

Follow the same recipe and method as for Granary Bread, but mix 3 tablespoons of fennel seeds in with the flour in step 1. Scatter the glazed loaves with fennel seeds instead of poppy or sesame seeds in step 9.

walnut BREAD

This bread is good on its own, but even better served with cheese. There are many ingredients which may be added with the walnuts to give extra flavour. Try 2 tablespoons raisins, 60 g (2 oz) chopped dried apricots, 60 g (2 oz) chopped skinned pistachios or 60 g (2 oz) chopped pitted prunes.

MAKES FOUR SMALL LOAVES

1 kg (2 lb) bag malted Granary flour
1 tablespoon salt
1½ tablespoons brown sugar
60 g (2 oz) fresh yeast
2 tablespoons walnut oil
600 ml (1 pint) warm water
125 g (4 oz) walnut halves

Follow Basic Method, adding 90 g (3 oz) chopped walnuts to dough at step 6. In step 10, bake for 10 mins at 200C (400F/Gas 6), reduce heat to 180C (350F/Gas 4) and cook for a further 25–30 min.

olive oil & rosemary BREAD

Extra yeast is used in this recipe to help the rising because of the olive oil, which retards the action of the yeast.

MAKES 48 ROLLS OR 2 LARGE LOAVES

1.4 kg (3 lb) strong white stone ground flour
1 tablespoon salt
2 tablespoons brown sugar
2 tablespoons chopped fresh rosemary
125 g (4 oz) fresh yeast
5 tablespoons extra virgin olive oil
800 ml (1½ pints) warm water

Follow Basic Method, adding chopped rosemary to flour, but omit stage 9. Half way through cooking brush bread with olive oil and sprinkle with a little extra chopped rosemary.

pissaladière

Pissaladière makes great picnic food. Transport it in the cooking tin, covered in foil to keep it warm. It also makes a wonderful accompaniment to Griddled Fillet of Angus Beef (page 53). Its strong, earthy flavours complement the beef beautifully. To speed preparation freeze a portion of uncooked bread dough for the base when making a batch of bread. Defrost at room temperature and allow it to prove a little before shaping into the tin. The stewed onion filling may also be prepared in advance and frozen for later use.

SERVES 4

250 g (9 oz) Granary bread dough (page 142)
1 quantity Stewed Shallots with Thyme (page 148) made with onions instead of shallots
2 tablespoons extra virgin olive oil
8 anchovy fillets
milk, for soaking
10 black olives

1   Make up bread dough as described on page 142.

2   Prepare onions as for Stewed Shallots with Thyme (page 148).

3   Preheat oven to 220C (425F/Gas 7).

4   Knock back dough and roll out to form a rectangle to fit a small roasting tin approximately 30 × 23 cm (12 × 9 inches). Press dough into corners with your fingers. Pinch up edges to form an attractive finish and to contain filling.

5   Bake bread base in preheated oven for 10 minutes. Remove from oven. Reduce temperature to 200C (400F/Gas 6).

6   Spoon onion mixture over base and drizzle with olive oil. Return to oven for a further 20 minutes, until dough is baked and onions have caramelised.

7   Soak anchovies in milk for a few minutes. Drain and rinse in cold water – this removes excessive saltiness. Cut olives in half, removing stones if necessary.

8   Scatter anchovies and olives over Pissaladière and return it to oven for 2 or 3 minutes to warm garnishes through.

9   Cut into finger shapes and serve.

mashed potatoes with olive oil

All potatoes are not the same! You must choose a good masher like Pentland Squire. Ask your greengrocer for advice.

SERVES 4

1 kg (2 lb 4 oz) Pentland Squire potatoes
2 teaspoons salt
2 tablespoons extra virgin olive oil
30 g (1 oz) unsalted butter
freshly grated nutmeg
freshly ground black pepper

1   Boil potatoes in large pan of salted water until cooked through. Drain well through a colander.

2   Return potatoes to pan and drive off any excess moisture over a low heat.

3   Mash potatoes by hand – do not use blender or food processor as this spoils texture of potatoes.

4   Add olive oil, butter, a generous grating of nutmeg and pepper. Beat well to make a fluffy mash. Serve hot

POTATO pancakes

Fill with spring onion and thyme, or aubergine and rosemary. Whatever the filling, surround the pancakes with a cream sauce, which they will absorb, becoming incredibly light and utterly memorable. This is based on a recipe by Georges Blanc.

SERVES 4

750 g (1½ lb) mashed potatoes with olive oil (see also previous recipe)
3 tablespoons self raising flour
3 eggs
3 tablespoons milk
3 tablespoons double cream
2 egg whites
salt and ground black pepper
freshly grated nutmeg
unsalted butter, for greasing

1   Mix mashed potatoes with flour, eggs, milk and double cream. Beat until smooth. Beat in egg whites and seasonings. Pass potato through a fine sieve into a clean bowl. Put to one side to rest.

2   Heat a griddle or skillet until evenly hot. Grease lightly. Drop teaspoons of mixture onto griddle – it should hold its shape straight away. Top with filling of your choice, then a little more potato batter to enclose filling.

3   Carefully lift pancake after about 1 minute – if the underside is golden, flip over and cook on second side.

pommes anna

This dish celebrates new potatoes. The one essential ingredient is a good waxy potato with a nutty flavour, such as Pink Fir Apple variety or Jersey Royal.

SERVES 4

1 kg (2 lb 4 oz) new potatoes
90 g (3 oz) unsalted butter

1   Preheat oven to 200C (400F/Gas 6).

2   Peel and thinly slice potatoes – use a mandolin if you have one. Melt butter.

3   To make 4 small Annas set four ring cutters on a baking tray. Dip potato slices in melted butter and build up layers within rings. Season layers lightly and push each down firmly with back of a fork or spoon, or a ramekin slightly smaller than the cutter.

4   Brush with any remaining butter. Bake in hot oven for 20 minutes, until potatoes are cooked through and Annas are golden brown. Test with a skewer.

5   Push potatoes through mould and invert onto serving dish – the undersides of the Annas will be the smoothest and most attractive.

bubble & squeak

SERVES 4

**550 g (1¼ lb) good mashing
potatoes**
30 g (1 oz) unsalted butter
**285 g (10 oz) dark green cabbage –
about half a small one**
1 small clove garlic
freshly grated nutmeg
salt and ground black pepper
1 tablespoon sunflower oil

1   Peel and chop potatoes.
Cook in a saucepan of boiling
salted water until soft. Drain well.
Mash with a potato ricer or a
masher and add half butter.

2   Remove outer leaves and
core from cabbage. Shred leaves
very finely. Crush garlic.

3   Melt remaining butter in a
large frying pan, add cabbage
and garlic and stir fry until soft.

4   Mix cabbage into mashed
potatoes, adding grated nutmeg
to taste. Season with salt and
pepper.

5   Form Bubble & Squeak into
four patty shapes. Heat the
remaining butter with oil in a
frying pan or skillet. Fry patties
for a few minutes on each side
until golden. Serve piping hot.

hot sesame
potato cakes

SERVES 4

1 kg (2 lb) floury potatoes
1 tablespoon double cream
4 tablespoons sesame seeds
1 red chilli
4 spring onions
1 lime
4 green cardamom pods
2 tablespoons sunflower oil
1 tablespoon sesame oil

1   Peel and chop potatoes. Boil
in a pan of salted water until
tender. Drain through a colander
and mash. Add cream.

2   Cut chilli in half – use one
half only. Remove seeds and
chop flesh very finely. Trim and
chop spring onions. Cook with
chilli in butter until soft.

3   Grate zest from one quarter
of lime. Crush cardamoms,
remove seeds and crush. Add
zest, seeds and vegetables to
potato. Season.

4   Form into cakes. Coat with
sesame seeds, pressing into
surface with a palette knife.

5   Heat the sunflower and
sesame oils in a frypan. Fry cakes
in hot oils until golden and crisp.
Drain on absorbent paper before
serving.

fragrant rice

*This is a good accompaniment to
Aubergine & Pumpkin Satay (page
81).*

SERVES 4

1 small onion
1 clove garlic
2 tablespoons sesame oil
180 g (6 oz) Thai rice
2 strips lemon zest
1 cinnamon stick
5 or 6 green cardamom pods
pinch saffron strands
1 teaspoon honey
**420 ml (15 fl oz) hot vegetable
stock (page 141)**
2 teaspoons salt
chopped fresh coriander

1   Finely chop half a small
onion. Crush garlic. Place in
saucepan with oil and cook
gently until softened but not
coloured.

2   Stir in rice and all seasonings
including honey. Break
cinnamon stick.

3   Add hot vegetable stock and
simmer gently for about 15
minutes, until cooked through.
Keep hot.

4   Just before serving remove
aromatics and stir in freshly
chopped coriander leaf to taste.

creamed POLENTA

All flours absorb different amounts of water, and so do different polentas. If the mixture appears too stiff, beat in some extra milk. The mixture should resemble fluffy mashed potatoes and should taste herby and slightly sweet. Adjust the seasoning if necessary. Beat a little double cream in at the last minute to make the polenta very light and fluffy.

SERVES 4

1 small onion
1 fat clove garlic
600 ml (1 pint) milk
300 ml (10 fl oz) single cream
4 tablespoons chopped fresh mixed herbs, to include thyme, sage, chives and a little rosemary
1 ramekin chopped fresh parsley
180 g (6 oz) quick-cook polenta
freshly ground black pepper
1 teaspoon salt

1   Peel onion and chop finely. Peel and crush garlic. Place both in a medium saucepan with milk and cream. Bring to boil and simmer until onion is soft.

2   Add herbs. Pour polenta into pan in a steady stream, stirring constantly. Beat well until smooth.

3   Cook over a low heat for 5 minutes, stirring continuously. Season to taste. Serve.

As a variation, beat in about 30 g (1 oz) grated Parmesan at the end of cooking.

POLENTA cakes

SERVES 4

1 small onion
1 fat clove garlic
600 ml (1 pint) milk
300 ml (10 fl oz) single cream
4 tablespoons chopped mixed herbs, to include parsley, chives, thyme and a little rosemary
180 g (6 oz) quick-cook polenta
30 g (1 oz) Gruyère cheese
1 large egg
1 teaspoon salt
freshly ground black pepper
½ teaspoon sugar

1   Peel onion and chop finely. Peel and crush garlic. Place in a medium saucepan with milk and cream. Bring to boil and simmer until onion is soft.

2   Add herbs. Pour polenta into pan in a steady stream, stirring constantly. Beat well until smooth.

3   Cook over a low heat for 5 minutes, stirring continuously. Mixture should resemble fluffy mashed potato.

4   Finely grate cheese and add to polenta with beaten egg. Add salt and pepper to taste and mix well.

5   Spread polenta 2.5–4 cm (1–1½ inches) thick in a baking tin. Chill in freezer for 30 minutes.

6   Cut into squares, or circles using a cutter.

7   Heat some good olive oil in a skillet or on a griddle. Cook polenta cakes on both sides until golden in colour and slightly puffed in appearance.

corncakes

A variation on drop scones, these little corncakes are very useful to serve with all kinds of savoury dishes. Vary the basic recipes by adding finely diced spring onion, chillies or a strong herb such as rosemary.

SERVES 4

2 tablespoons plain flour
1 egg
2 tablespoons double cream
salt and ground black pepper
250 g (9 oz) corn kernels

1   Blend flour in a mixing bowl with egg, cream and seasonings. Add half corn kernels. Purée in a blender or food processor until smooth.

2   Return mixture to bowl and stir in remaining corn kernels.

3   Heat a griddle or heavy based frying pan to an even medium heat. Grease with a smearing of butter.

4   Drop teaspoonfuls of mixture onto griddle and cook for 2–3 minutes until golden brown on the underside.

5   Flip over with a palette knife and cook on the second side. The cakes will puff up and cook to a golden, lacy finish.

You can use canned or frozen sweetcorn kernels for this recipe.

FRESH saffron PASTA

If you have a pasta machine, roll out the paste on No. 6 setting.

Keep remaining saffron infusion in the refrigerator and use in pasta, poultry or rice dishes. It will keep for several weeks.

SERVES 4

2 packets saffron stamens
6 tablespoons water
300 g (10 oz) plain flour
pinch salt
1 whole egg
4 egg yolks
2 tablespoons extra virgin olive oil

1   Steep saffron in the water. Place flour, salt and egg and egg yolks in a food processor and mix briefly to blend. Add oil and 2 tablespoons saffron infusion through feed tube. Process until just binding together.

2   Knead on a lightly floured surface until paste is smooth. Cover in plastic wrap and chill for at least 1 hour.

3   To make tagliatelle: use a quarter of the paste at a time. Roll out very thinly on a lightly floured surface. Cut into strips about 60 cm (24 inches) long and allow to dry slightly. Fold ends of strips to middle, repeat twice more.

4   Cut down in quite fine strips along folded length with a long bladed knife. Carefully unfold and dry over a rolling pin or new broom handle suspended between work tops. Allow to dry for 30 minutes.

5   Shape as you need and cook briefly, for about 1 minute, in boiling, salted water.

hazelnut PASTA

We developed this pasta to help bring variety to vegetarian dishes at the Old Vicarage.

SERVES 4

60 g (2 oz) hazelnuts
300 g (10 oz) plain flour
pinch salt
1 egg
3 egg yolks
water, to mix

1   Roast hazelnuts in a hot oven at 200C (400F/Gas 6) for a few minutes until they are golden and skins come off easily. Rub off skins with a clean cloth. Place in a clean coffee grinder or food processor.

2   Place hazelnuts, flour, salt, egg and egg yolks in a food processor and mix briefly to blend.

3   Add a little water at a time and process until just binding together. This mixing may be done just as easily by hand in a mixing bowl.

4   Knead on a lightly floured surface until paste is smooth and shiny. Cover in plastic wrap and put to rest in refrigerator for at least 1 hour, or until required.

spinach PASTA

SERVES 4

SPINACH & WATERCRESS PUREE:
generous bunch watercress
250 g (9 oz) fresh spinach

300 g (10 oz) plain flour
pinch salt
1 egg
3 egg yolks
1 tablespoon extra virgin olive oil
flour, to dust

1   Prepare purée. Wash watercress and spinach. Shake off excess water. Purée in blender or food processor with 2 or 3 tablespoons water. Use machine at low speed.

2   Heat purée gently in a saucepan until very bright green in colour with liquid separating off.

3   Drain through muslin or a fine linen teatowel, squeezing the pulp to remove all excess liquid. The resulting pulp is now ready to colour and flavour pasta.

4   Prepare pasta. You will need 1 tablespoon – freeze the rest. Place flour, 1 tablespoon of purée, salt, egg and egg yolks in a food processor and mix briefly to blend.

5   Add olive oil and process until just binding together. This mixing may be done just as easily by hand in a mixing bowl.

6   Knead on a lightly floured surface until paste is smooth and shiny. Cover in plastic wrap and put to pasta rest in refrigerator for at least 1 hour, or until required.

pickled plums

These make an excellent accompaniment to game. Pickle when plums are in season and plentiful.

MAKES 1.4 KG (3 LB)
1 kg (2lb 4 oz) caster sugar
300 ml (10 fl oz) red wine vinegar
150 ml (5 fl oz) ruby port
1 lemon
1 level teaspoon coriander seeds
1 cinnamon stick, broken into pieces
5 cm (2 inch) piece fresh root ginger
3 whole cloves
1.4 kg (3 lb) firm red plums

1   Place sugar in a large saucepan with vinegar and port. Pare rind from lemon. Lightly crush coriander seeds. Peel ginger and chop roughly. Add flavourings to pan with cloves. Heat gently until sugar is dissolved. Bring to boil, then simmer for 5 minutes.

2   Cut plums in half and remove stones. Lay cut side up in 2 or 3 shallow flameproof casseroles.

3   Pour boiling sweet vinegar over plums. Heat to return liquor to boil. (This may be done in a hot oven if you do not have flameproof casseroles). Remove from heat. Leave overnight.

4   The next day, remove plums from liquor with a slotted spoon. Pack into 4 sterile jars.

5   Heat liquor and aromatics and pour over plums. Cover and seal while still hot.

6   Label and keep for 2–3 weeks before using.

mulled pears

It is worth making more than you need of these. They keep well in the refrigerator and may be served with game or other meat dishes. They are particularly good with Fillet of Fallow Deer (see page 80). Putting juniper berries back into the sauce looks very effective.

SERVES 12

6 Conference pears
300 ml (10 fl oz) red wine, something soft like a Merlot
150 ml (5 fl oz) ruby port
2 cinnamon sticks
1 lemon
3 cloves
10 juniper berries
1 tablespoon sugar
chilled unsalted butter, to finish

1   Choose a small pan, so that pears will be covered by wine.

2   Peel, core and cut pears in half.

3   Bring wine and port to boil. Break cinnamon sticks and add with the lemon, cloves, juniper berries and sugar. Lower in pears. Simmer gently until just tender. Transfer to a bowl and leave overnight in refrigerator for pears to take on deep red colour of wine right through.

4   To serve, remove the cinnamon, lemon, cloves and juniper berries. Reheat pears in small amount of spiced wine. Keep hot.

5   Warm remaining mulled wine and whisk in chilled butter to make glossy, thickened sauce.

6   Pour sauce over warm pears.

STEWED shallots WITH THYME

This 'marmalade' has several uses; a sweet relish for roast beef, a topping for yeast dough, a tart filling with anchovies and olives, or baked in filo pastry as a strudel.

MAKES 1 KG (2 LB 4 OZ)

1 kg (2 lb 4 oz) shallots or red onions
4 tablespoons extra virgin olive oil
2 tablespoons wine or sherry vinegar
2 tablespoons amontillado sherry
2 tablespoons brown sugar
4 stems fresh thyme
salt and ground black pepper

1   Peel shallots or onions and slice very thinly. Cook slowly in a large frying pan with olive oil until softened but not coloured. Add wine vinegar, bring to boiling point and boil until evaporated.

2   Stir in sherry, brown sugar, thyme and seasoning, stirring until sugar is dissolved.

3   Reduce heat to a slow simmer. Cook shallots until caramelised, when liquid will mostly have evaporated. Mixture will be golden, syrupy and sticky.

4   Remove thyme stems. Pick leaves from 2 or 3 extra stems and stir into shallots. Season to taste.

avocado salsa

I serve this with the Caramelised & Roasted Tomato Tarts (page 82).

SERVES 4

1 shallot
1 fat clove garlic
2 tablespoons extra virgin olive oil
4 spring onions
2 limes
2 small avocados
1 red chilli
1 green chilli
3 tomatoes
2 pieces stem ginger
1 teaspoon sugar
2 tablespoons walnut oil
fresh coriander
1 tablespoon chopped fresh chives
salt and ground black pepper

1   Finely chop shallot and crush garlic. Cook in olive oil until soft but not browned.

2   Trim and chop spring onions. Grate zest from limes and squeeze juice. Peel and chop avocados and toss flesh in lime juice. Cut chillies in half, use half of each and chop flesh very finely.

3   Skin tomatoes, remove seeds and dice flesh.

4   Finely chop stem ginger. Remove pan from heat and add ginger to onion with all remaining prepared vegetables and seasonings. Add freshly chopped coriander, season and use as required within 24 hours.

crab apple & thyme JELLY

Nothing could be simpler than Crab Apple Jelly. Set up a jelly bag – if you haven't got one, it is very easy to improvise. You will need 1.25 metres (1½ yards) of butter muslin, folded in two. Upturn a kitchen stool on a table and tie the four corners of the muslin, one to each leg of the stool. Stand a wide mixing bowl on the seat to catch the liquid – voila! One jelly bag!

MAKES ABOUT 2.2 kg (5 lb)

1.8 kg (4 lb) crab apples
1.7 litre (3 pints) water
450 g (1 lb) caster sugar to each 600 ml (1 pint) liquid
good bunch fresh thyme, including some flowering heads

1   Wash and dry crab apples. Cut in half. Leave skins and pips as they help to colour and set jelly. Place in a preserving pan or large saucepan.

2   Cover fruits with water.

3   Bring to boil, then simmer for about 30 minutes, until apples have fallen to a soft pulp.

4   Pour pulp into jelly bag and leave to strain overnight. Do not push pulp through or squeeze bag – it will result in a cloudy jelly. It is not something you can hurry – rather like drinking a good bottle of claret!

5   Wash five 450 g (1 lb) jam jars in hot soapy water, rinse thoroughly and place in a low oven to dry.

6   Measure liquid. Allow 450g (1 lb) sugar to every 600 ml (1 pint).

7   Dissolve sugar in liquid in a preserving pan or large saucepan. Bring slowly to boil and keep at a rolling boil for about 20 minutes.

8   After 15 minutes add several sprigs of thyme and start testing for a set. Use a long handled wooden spoon to stir jelly. Turn spoon with back of spoon facing you. Wait until liquid flakes down back of spoon and drips off, leaving a long, blobby drip like an icicle which adheres to spoon. This will give you a set.

9   Remove thyme stems. Pour jelly into warm jars and cover with a waxed disc.

10   Allow to cool for about 30 minutes. Remove wax discs and drop in thyme leaves and flowers. Stir gently with tip of a clean knife to disperse thyme through jelly. Top again with waxed discs.

11   Cover pots with lids or cellophane. Label and store in a cool, dry place.

tomato & chilli

SALSA

This is a textured sauce with 'chunky bits' and fire from chillies.

SERVES 4

1 shallot
1 fat clove garlic
1 hot red chilli
14 ripe tomatoes
3 tablespoons extra virgin olive oil
½ small red pepper
150 ml (5 fl oz) fish stock (page 140)
½ teaspoon caster sugar
1 tablespoon tomato purée or passata
salt and ground black pepper
Tabasco
chopped fresh coriander

1   Finely chop shallot and crush garlic. Finely chop flesh of half chilli.

2   Skin tomatoes (see page 48). Cut tomatoes in half and remove core and seeds. Chop tomato flesh, reserving two tomatoes for garnish.

3   Heat olive oil in a medium pan, add shallot, garlic and red chilli and cook until soft. Finely chop flesh red pepper.

4   Add chopped tomatoes, stock, sugar, tomato purée or passata, salt, pepper and Tabasco and cook until soft. Purée until smooth in a blender or food processor. Return to pan.

5   Chop reserved tomatoes and add to sauce with coriander. Heat through gently. Taste sauce and adjust seasoning.

tapenade

Tapenade is a paste or paté of olives. It has a pungent flavour, so use it only in small amounts to give an authentic Provençale flavour to your cooking. Store in the refrigerator. Tapenade spread on crostini (toasted crusty bread rubbed with garlic and olive oil) makes a good savoury snack with wine. It goes particularly well with a glass of chilled fino.

SERVES 4

1 teaspoon capers
1 clove garlic
30 black olives
4 anchovies fillets in oil
1 teaspoon lemon juice
¼ teaspoon Dijon mustard
freshly ground black pepper
about 6 tablespoons extra virgin olive oil

1   Drain capers well on absorbent kitchen paper. Crush garlic.

2   Blend all ingredients together in a pestle and mortar except the olive oil, or purée in a blender or food processor.

3   Gradually add enough oil to make a thick, spreadable paste. Taste and adjust seasoning.

cucumber relish

This relish balances beautifully with Spiced Fillet of Beef with Hot Smoked Peppers (page 17).

SERVES 4

½ small cucumber
salt
1 small clove garlic
extra virgin olive oil
1 tablespoon white wine vinegar
3 dessertspoons sunflower oil
½ teaspoon sugar
white pepper

1   Peel cucumber and scoop out seeds using a teaspoon. Cut cucumber into fine slices. Layer slices in a colander and salt lightly to draw out juices. Leave for 15 minutes.

2   Prepare relish dressing. Crush garlic and mix with olive oil, white wine vinegar, sunflower oil and sugar. Season with salt and white pepper.

3   Rinse cucumber in plenty of running water. Pat dry on absorbent kitchen paper. Place cucumber in serving bowl and pour dressing over, seasoning dressing if necessary. Chill until ready to serve.

soy & cinnamon sauce

SERVES 4

2 tablespoons dark soy sauce
150 ml (5 fl oz) vegetable stock
(see page 141)
1 tablespoon amontillado sherry
1 cinnamon stick
1 tablespoon coriander seeds
30 g (1 oz) unsalted butter, chilled
1 tablespoon chopped fresh
coriander

1   Place soy sauce, stock, sherry, cinnamon stick (broken in half), and coriander seeds in a small pan and boil to reduce by half to concentrate flavour.

2   Pass through a fine sieve into a clean pan.

3   Cut the butter into small pieces and gradually whisk into pan, until a thickened glossy sauce is formed.

4   Add chopped coriander just before serving.

oregano sauce

SERVES 4

150 ml (5 fl oz) double cream
150 ml (5 fl oz) reduced fish stock
(page 140)
3 sprigs fresh oregano
fresh chives
½ teaspoon lemon juice
salt and ground black pepper

1   Boil cream in a saucepan until reduced by half and thickened. Add fish stock and heat through.

2   Finely chop fresh herbs. Stir into sauce with lemon juice and check seasoning. Serve with Hot Smoked Sea Bass (page 84).

rocket pureé

This makes an excellent sauce for Caramelised & Roasted Tomato Tarts (page 82).

SERVES 4

1 small onion
4 tablespoons crême fraîche
1 bunch rocket or watercress
salt and ground black pepper

1   Use only one quarter of a small onion – chop it finely. Cook onion in crême fraîche in a small pan until soft.

2   Bring to boil. Plunge in rocket or watercress, remove immediately from heat and purée in a blender or food processor.

3   Rinse pan. Pass sauce through fine sieve back into pan and season to taste.

4   Reheat gently when required.

smoked pepper salsa

Serve with Hazelnut Toasted Goat's Cheese & Tomato Bruschetta (page 48).

SERVES 4

1 red pepper
1 yellow pepper
1 green pepper
large sprig of rosemary
1 small onion
1 clove garlic
1 red chilli
4 tablespoons extra virgin olive oil
2 teaspoons balsamic vinegar
salt and ground black pepper
1 tablespoon chopped fresh chives

1   Roast and skin peppers (see page 30). Cut peppers in half. Remove core, seeds and membrane.

2   Set up a smoker (see page 25). Place some rosemary in base. Place peppers in smoker. Smoke for 2 minutes.

4   Peel onion and chop finely. Peel and crush garlic. Remove core and seeds from chilli and chop finely. Heat 1 tablespoon olive oil in a pan, add onion, garlic and chilli and cook until softened.

5   Whisk together remaining oil, vinegar and seasonings in a medium bowl. Add fried onion mixture and chives.

6   Cut smoked pepper halves into thick strips and add to bowl. Stir all ingredients together carefully and season to taste.

7   Leave salsa to stand, to allow flavours to blend. Store in refrigerator for up to 7 days.

brandy snap BASKETS

Make the brandy snap mixture the day before you need it. The snaps are thinner and crisper if the mixture is at least a day old.

MAKES 4

125 g (4 oz) unsalted butter
4 tablespoons golden syrup
125 g (4 oz) dark brown sugar
125 g (4 oz) plain flour
1 level teaspoon ground ginger
2 lemons or 4 small pudding basins, for moulding

1   Heat butter, syrup and sugar in a pan over a low heat until melted. Sieve together flour and ginger. Add to mixture in pan and beat until smooth. Cool and chill until ready for use.

2   Preheat oven to 160C (325F/Gas 3). Lightly grease a baking tray.

3   Place walnut-sized pieces of mixture onto the baking sheet. Spread into circles.

4   Bake in preheated oven for 5–7 minutes. Remove from oven and allow to settle for a minute or so.

5   Lift biscuits from tin with a palette knife and drape each one over half a lemon or small pudding mould, squeezing into a tulip shape while still warm. Repeat to make four cups. Leave to cool, then remove from moulds.

6   Store in an air-tight tin. Serve filled with homemade ice cream.

praline boxes

MAKES 4–5 BOXES

30 g (1 oz) hazelnuts
125 g (4 oz) caster sugar

1   Roast hazelnuts in a hot oven at 200C (400F/Gas 6) for a few minutes until they are golden and skins come off easily. Rub off skins with a clean cloth.

2   Make a caramel by dissolving sugar in 4 tablespoons water in a small pan. Bring to boil and fast boil to a golden caramel colour. Pour caramel over hazelnuts on an oiled baking tray. Leave until cold and brittle.

3   Grind praline to a coarse powder in a grinder or crush between sheets of baking parchment with a rolling pin. Spread powder evenly and thinly on a baking sheet.

4   Bake in preheated oven for 9–11 minutes, or until a glassy sheet of praline is formed. Remove from oven and cool slightly.

5   Work quickly. Cut into square shapes of approximately 6 cm (2.5 inches). You will need five pieces for each box. Any left-over trimmings can be reground and reused.

6   Join the pieces of praline together by melting the edges slightly either with a blow torch or a hot skewer. It is best to lay the first square down flat.

7   Fill with ice cream when required. Balance a fifth square on top to resemble an opening lid.

OLD VIC foolproof pastry

Use a whole 250 g packet of butter and a whole 250 g packet of white cooking fat. Divide the pastry dough into three and freeze two pieces for later use. Freezing the pastry before it is cooked does it no harm at all. Allow to defrost slowly.

2 egg yolks
1 egg
1 tablespoon lemon juice
6 tablespoons iced water
250 g (9 oz) butter
250 g (9 oz) white vegetable shortening
670 g (1½ lb) plain flour
1 tablespoon icing sugar
1½ teaspoons salt

1   Beat together the egg yolks, egg, lemon juice and water and chill in the refrigerator – this will thicken the liquid slightly.

2   Cut fats into small dice. Sieve flour and icing sugar together into a large mixing bowl.

3   Rub fats into flour mixture to make a fine crumb – use only your fingertips.

4   Add all liquid at once. Stir until mixture starts to bind – finish with your hand.

5   Knead gently on a lightly floured surface. Cover pastry in plastic wrap and leave to rest for about 1 hour in refrigerator. Roll out as required.

almond tuilles

We serve these light biscuits at The Old Vicarage with Cinnamon Ice Cream (page 154). The biscuits should be in the shape of a roof tile (hence the name) so they are draped over rolling pins when still warm, to take on a curved shape. If the biscuits become too brittle before you can remove them from the baking sheet, just pop them back in the oven for a few seconds to soften. They will become very crisp and brittle when cold.

Use finely chopped almonds if slivered are not available. Spare mixture may be frozen for later use.

MAKES 24

90 g (3 oz) plain flour
60 g (2 oz) ground almonds
150 g (5 oz) icing sugar
2 eggs
2 egg whites
45 g (1½ oz) slivered almonds

1   Sieve together flour, ground almonds and icing sugar into a mixing bowl.

2   Lightly whisk eggs and egg whites together with a fork and pour into bowl. Using a spatula, draw dry ingredients into eggs to make a batter. Put aside to rest for 30 minutes. Preheat oven to 180C (350F/Gas 4).

3   Lightly grease 2 totally flat baking sheets. Spoon no more than 3 separate tablespoons of mixture onto each baking sheet – the biscuits will spread considerably during baking. Use back of spoon to smooth mixture into oval shapes about 5 × 7.5 cm (2 × 3 inches). Scatter a few slivered almonds over each biscuit.

4   Bake for about 4 minutes, until edges of biscuits turn pale golden. Stand for 30 seconds on baking sheet then remove biscuits with a flexible palette knife and drape over a rolling pin to set.

5   Continue baking biscuits, 6 at a time, until mixture is finished.

6   Dredge with icing sugar before serving.

coffee SAUCE

This sauce requires double strength coffee. Use a full bodied filter coffee such as Mocha or Costa Rica/Java, and make it with half the quantity of water normally required.

SERVES 4

2 eggs
90 g (3 oz) caster sugar
150 ml (5 fl oz) double strength coffee
2 tablespoons cognac
150 ml (5 fl oz) double cream

1   Whisk eggs and sugar together in a bowl until thick.

2   Pour into a saucepan with coffee and cook over a gentle heat until sauce thickens, stirring constantly.

3   Stir in cognac.

4   Whisk double cream lightly and fold into sauce to give an aerated texture.

5   Serve immediately.

brandy cream

This is a traditional sauce for Christmas Pudding and is served at The Old Vicarage at Christmas time.

SERVES 10

420 ml (15 fl oz) double cream
4 tablespoons brandy
1 tablespoon icing sugar

1   Whisk all ingredients together in a large bowl until a soft floppy consistency is achieved. Chill until required.

butterscotch SAUCE

We serve this with Pear Shortcake (page 136) but it's wonderful over vanilla ice-cream too.

SERVES 4

60 g (2 oz) caster sugar
1 tablespoon brandy
150 ml (5 fl oz) double cream
90 g (3 oz) unsalted butter
natural vanilla essence

1   Heat sugar with 2 tablespoons water in a small pan until dissolved. Bring to boil and boil rapidly until sugar syrup turns golden and forms a caramel.

2   Quickly whisk in remaining ingredients and keep whisking over a low heat until a smooth, golden, buttery sauce is made. Serve warm.

blackberry ICE CREAM

Really a frozen parfait, this ice cream is simplicity itself to make.

Use whilst still easy to scoop or allow to soften slightly in the fridge for 30 minutes before serving.

SERVES 4

1 kg (2 lb 4 oz) fresh blackberries
1 tablespoon lemon juice
2 tablespoons caster sugar
8 egg whites
180 g (6 oz) icing sugar
600 ml (1 pint) double cream

1   Cook the blackberries, lemon juice and caster sugar together in a saucepan until fruit is soft. Press through a sieve to extract seeds.

2   Return to pan and reduce to concentrate flavour and drive off excess liquid. The purée should be thick. Allow to cool. Chill.

3   Whisk egg whites in a large bowl with a pinch of salt until stiff peaks form. Gradually fold in icing sugar and whisk again to stiff glossy peaks.

4   Whisk cream in a bowl to a soft, flopping consistency. Fold in chilled fruit purée.

5   Fold in meringue mixture using a hand whisk and taking care to keep mixture light but evenly mixed.

6   Pour into a 2 litre shallow freezer container and freeze until firm.

caramel ICE CREAM

This is delicious served with Coffee Sauce (page 153). For the very adventurous cook, try serving in Praline Boxes (page 152).

SERVES 4

750 ml (1½ pint) single cream
10 egg yolks
2 tablespoons vanilla sugar
1 level teaspoon cornflour
300 ml (10 fl oz) double cream
100 g (4 oz) caster sugar

1   Pour single cream into a saucepan and bring to boil.

2   Cream egg yolks, vanilla sugar and cornflour together in a bowl. Gradually add hot cream, whisking continuously.

3   Rinse pan and return mixture to it. Cook gently over a low heat until custard will thickly coat back of a spoon. Strain through a sieve into a bowl and allow to cool.

4   Make a caramel by dissolving sugar in 4 tablespoons water in a small pan. Bring to boil and fast boil to a golden caramel colour. Quickly whisk caramel into custard. Allow to cool.

5   Whisk double cream in a bowl until floppy. Fold into cooled custard.

6   Freeze. Use an ice cream maker which will churn mixture to increase volume and give a lighter ice cream. Alternately freeze in a shallow freezer container and whisk after 3 hours to double the bulk. Freeze again and repeat process a second time.

cinnamon ICE CREAM

A truly gorgeous ice cream served with Caramelised Apple Balls.

SERVES 4

10 egg yolks
1 level teaspoon cornflour
225 g (8 oz) vanilla sugar
750 ml (1½ pint) single cream
3 cinnamon sticks
600 ml (1 pint) double cream

1   Blend egg yolks, cornflour and sugar together in a bowl with a little single cream.

2   Pour remaining cream into a saucepan. Break cinnamon sticks into cream. Bring to boil. Pour onto egg mixture, whisking constantly.

3   Rinse pan and return custard to it. Cook gently over a low heat, stirring constantly, until custard coats back of a wooden spoon. Allow to cool.

4   Whisk double cream until soft and floppy. Fold into cooled custard.

5   Strain custard into an ice cream maker and proceed as directed, or freeze, whisking every 2–3 hours, until completely set.

CARAMELISED apple balls

This is an unusual but edible decoration which we serve with ice-cream or apple desserts. Choose a firm-textured, tart eating apple for the best contrast in tastes.

3 eating apples
2 tablespoons caster sugar
15 g (½ oz) unsalted butter

1   Peel apples and use a melon baller to scoop balls from fruit.

2   Place caster sugar in a small pan with 2 tablespoons water. Heat gently until sugar is dissolved. Boil rapidly until golden in colour. Add butter.

3   Drop apple balls into caramel and cook briefly until just soft, but retaining their shape.

4   Serve ice cream in scoops with apple balls and caramel spooned over.

passion fruit
ICE CREAM

This is a very simple ice cream but it must be made with fresh free-range eggs and used within a couple of days of making. I'm sure that will be no hardship!

SERVES 4

8 passion fruits
45 g (1½ oz) caster sugar
300 ml (10 fl oz) double cream
4 free-range eggs
100 g (4 oz) icing sugar

1   Make purée. Cut passion fruits in half and remove pulp with a teaspoon.

2   Purée pulp in a blender or food processor then sieve out seeds.

3   Cook purée in a small pan with measured sugar and reduce to a thickened pulp with the consistency of custard. Allow to cool, then chill well.

4   Whisk cream in a large bowl to a soft floppy consistency. Separate eggs and stir in yolks.

5   Whisk egg whites until stiff in another bowl, then whisk in icing sugar to make a meringue.

6   Fold fruit purée into cream mixture. Using a balloon whisk fold meringue into cream mixture. Always add lighter mixture to heavier – that way you do not break down volume.

7   Pour into shallow freezer container and freeze until set. The mixture will not require whisking or stirring during freezing.

lemon curd ICE CREAM

For Lemon Curd Ice Cream (ideal served with Mascarpone Cheesecake, page 98) omit passion fruit purée in Passion Fruit Ice Cream recipe (see left) and use 4 tablespoons Lemon Curd.

lemon curd

MAKES

3 lemons, preferably unwaxed
120 g (4 oz) unsalted butter
180 g (6 oz) caster sugar
3 eggs

1   Wash and dry lemons – use hot water to remove any wax treatment they may have been given. Grate zests and squeeze juice.

2   Place butter, sugar, lemon zest and half lemon juice in top of a double boiler or in a bowl which will fit on a pan of water. Heat until butter is melted.

3   Beat eggs and add to mixture. Cook gently, stirring constantly, until thickened. This is a very satisfying job and allows you to relax and think beautiful thoughts! It cannot be rushed.

4   Stir in remaining juice and continue cooking – total time will be 15–20 minutes. The curd should thickly coat back of a spoon. Run your forefinger through curd. It should leave a clear, clean trail.

5   Pass curd through a fine sieve to remove any traces of egg white. Use immediately or pour into clean, sterile pots (see page 149). Cover and keep in refrigerator.

index

Tessa Bramley's restaurant is
The Old Vicarage
Ridgeway Moor
Ridgeway
Sheffield S12 3XW
England
Telephone 0742 475 814
Fax 0742 477 079